W.R.V.Brade

THE PSYCHOLOGICAL TEACHING
OF ST. AUGUSTINE

THE PSYCHOLOGICAL TEACHING OF ST. AUGUSTINE

BY

JAMES MORGAN, D.D.

Author of " THE IMPORTANCE OF
TERTULLIAN IN THE DEVELOPMENT
OF CHRISTIAN DOGMA."

LONDON : ELLIOT STOCK
PUBLISHER
(*Props.:* SIDNEY KIEK & SON, LTD.)
2 PATERNOSTER BUILDINGS, E.C.

Made in England

PREFACE

SCANNING the catalogue of one of our great public libraries, the student would conclude that all that could be written about St. Augustine and his teaching had already been recorded. It seems presumptuous, therefore, to add further to this multitude of volumes by the issue of another contribution dealing with this illustrious scholar. A study of the list of those already issued, however, will reveal the fact that hardly anything, up to the present time, has been written on the remarkable psychological teaching of this Father of the Church, and although I have no special qualification for undertaking such an important subject, yet I venture to present to the reader some results of an examination of this aspect of St. Augustine's teaching, in the hope that it may stir up interest and lead to a deeper appreciation of the genius of this African Father and also inspire others more competent than myself to develop this branch of study and advance it to the position which it merits.

The list of books referred to in the Bibliography contains the titles of those volumes which I have found most valuable in my study of this subject, and I am indebted to the various authors whose works I have endeavoured to acknowledge.

My grateful thanks are due to two friends who have been most kind in offering suggestions in the compilation of this volume. Dr. Lonsdale Ragg has kindly read through the MSS. and given helpful suggestions, and Dr. C. H. Valentine has made some useful comments on the chapters that deal with the soul and with the epistemology of St. Augustine. Without their encouragement I should not have ventured to publish in book form the result of my studies.

It would be ungrateful on my part if I omitted to acknowledge the kind help of Miss N. S. Graham for her assistance in compiling the index and in reading the proofs.

CONTENTS

INTRODUCTION

THE greatness of Augustine as thinker, writer, theologian, defender of the faith, and saint, is universally recognised. He is the most commanding personality of the ancient Church, perhaps of the Church in any age. In importance, he takes rank inferior to no teacher who has laboured in her service since the days of the Apostles. Augustine is not only the greatest of the Church Fathers and the Prince of Theologians, but he is also a philosopher of the first rank who fused the finest elements of Greek and Roman thought into a great and enduring synthesis.

In St. Augustine we see the three elements of a well-balanced religion, the personal, the institutional, and the intellectual triumphantly combined. Dr. Glover writes of him: "He gave to Christian thought on God and man, on sin and grace, on the world and the Church, an impulse and a direction, the force of which is still unspent. He shaped the Catholic theory of the Church, he gave the great Popes the idea of the City of God, God's Empire, he was the father of the mystics, the founder of the scholastic philosophy of the Middle Ages, and above all the hero and master of the Renaissance and the Reformation. He gave Calvin the doctrine of Predestination, and he was the only Father from whom Luther really learnt.[1]

Another writer says of him: "He is the highest point of the development of the Western Church before the Middle Ages. From him the Mysticism, no less than the Scholasticism, of the Middle Ages has drawn its life; he forms the mightiest pillar of Roman Catholicism and the leaders of the Reformation derived from his writings,

[1] Glover. *Life and Letters in the Fourth Century*, p. 194.

9

next to the study of the Holy Scriptures, those principles which gave birth to a new era[1].

It is important to note the many formative influences that were focused on this African Father. Semitic influences were transmitted through the society, perhaps through the blood, of the Phœnicians, whose language and traditions were still alive and familiar to him. Persian influences were brought to bear on him by Manichæism, in which he became involved. Latin and Greek writers influenced him during his youth; he specially studied the writings of Vergil, Plotinus, and Plato. His father, his nurses and his tutors helped to form his character. We can understand the nature of the gentle and persistent teaching of his mother and especially her noble example, which made its appeal to his great heart and to his great mind[2].

One other writer, Gustav Krüger, may be quoted: "Of the four great Fathers of the Church he was admittedly the greatest—more profound than Ambrose, his spiritual father, more original and systematic than Jerome, his correspondent, and intellectually far more distinguished than Gregory the Great, his pupil on the Papal throne. The theological position and influence of Augustine may be said to be unrivalled. No single name has ever exercised such power over the Christian Church, and no one mind ever made so deep an impression upon Christian thought. In him scholastics and mystics, popes and the opponents of the papal supremacy, have seen their champion. He was the fulcrum on which Luther rested the thoughts by which he sought to lift the past of the Church out of the rut; yet the judgment of Catholics still proclaims the

[1] C. Bindemann. *Der helige Augustinus*.
[2] See Chapter by J. B. Reeves in *A Monument to St. Augustine*.

ideas of Augustine as the only sound basis of philosophy[1].

Although Augustine was a man of the greatest originality, he was, nevertheless, an indefatigable student, who was greatly influenced by all that he read. In the writings of his early years he seldom mentions the names of the authors he had studied most, but their influence is everywhere evident. He was one of those men who never read a book without subsequently betraying the fact either in their conversation or in their writings. Although it was natural for him to use illustrations, and quite unnecessary for him to borrow from others, yet we cannot but suspect at times that in his writings there are reminiscences of illustrations which he had found in writings or in the course of his experience. The various individual references and the general style of *De Ordine*, chap. IV, remind us of sections of the *De Officiis* of his master, Ambrosius.

Many scholars have over-estimated the importance of Augustine's dependence on Plato and Plotinus. It is true that many of his pages reflect the influence of these philosophers, but it is our duty to prove that he has not followed them slavishly; he has also been indebted to Aristotle, a fact which has been neglected by many writers on Augustine. Someone has well remarked that Augustine is like a great bumble bee, finding an entrance into every flower in the garden of philosophy, and coming out again covered with the fruitful pollen which he cannot help scattering wherever he goes. The borrowed material is, however, the basis of new and varied thoughts, full of life; everything is transformed through the operation of his transcendent genius.

[1] Gustav Krüger. Art. *Augustine* in Ency. Brit.

Thimme's remarks are worth repeating: "With earnestness and determination he confined himself to practical questions of importance, and questions which theory did not despair of answering. There is nothing dreamy and Gnostic-like in his thinking. He is by no means tempted to follow Plotinus in his fantastic and abstract speculations about the 'Nous', the world-soul, etc. His instinct for knowledge springs from a burning desire to attain to complete certainty on the greatest questions."[1]

Augustine was a man of keen spiritual insight; he was also a profound philosopher. He affirmed that his mind preferred nothing to the discovery of truth. It is in keeping, therefore, with the Augustinian spirit and mode of procedure to approach our task from the purely intellectual standpoint, from the philosophical and psychological rather than from a purely religious point of view.

St. Augustine is the greatest teacher of all the Patristic philosophers, and one of the most profound thinkers of all times. He was first and foremost a theologian, and perhaps the greatest of them all. His chief interest centred in the development, exposition, and defence of Christian dogma. Theology, in his opinion, occupies the highest rank in the hierarchy of the sciences. The value of all human knowledge is to be reckoned in terms of the service it renders to the science of God. To know God is the most desirable good in life. It is in this knowledge only that man can find true happiness. The man who is versed in all human sciences, but does not know God, is indeed miserable; but if he knows God, though he be ignorant of

[1] Thimme. *Augustins geistige Entwickelung in den ersten Jahren nach seiner.*

all else, he is happy[1]. Referring to Philosophy in particular he observed that the unique aim of true and genuine philosophy is to aid man in his quest for knowledge of the Uncaused Cause of all things.[2]

From the works of St. Augustine, considered as a whole, we receive the impression that his rich contributions of thought are directed into two different channels and that they coalesce only as the result of the remarkable personality of this great teacher.

It is necessary to distinguish the philosophy of St. Augustine from his theology. As a theologian, Augustine in all his investigations, keeps the conception of the Church clearly in mind, as a criterion. But, when he writes as a philosopher, he represents all his ideas as centres about the principle of the absolute and immediate certainty of consciousness. Because St. Augustine treats of all his problems in reference to their twofold relation to these accepted postulates, all the questions he tries to answer are most suggestive.

We may compare St. Augustine's system of thought to an elliptic which is formed by revolution about two centres; we must remember, however, that this inner duality leads frequently to contradiction. It is a remarkable fact that this great teacher himself, in the course of his development, transferred the emphasis of his teaching more and more from the philosophical to the theological centre. We recognise this fact in his backward look over his own literary activity. The *Retractations*, which evidence his remarkable candour, explain and modify his former teaching. In them he sometimes acknowledges even his mistakes of opinion.

[1] *Conf.*, v, 4.
[2] *De Ord.*, II, v, 16.

St. Augustine was a philosopher before he became a theologian. His philosophy anticipates, to a remarkable degree, the standpoint of modern thought. For example, the modern development of thought, beginning with Descartes, fails to recognise objective knowledge as a starting-point, and, accordingly, refers to the principle of self as the clue to the interpretation of reality. This system of teaching has its counterpart, often most satisfactorily, in the writings of St. Augustine.

St. Augustine and Descartes lay remarkable emphasis on the nature of the "self" as an active will, in opposition to the intellectualism which characterised ancient philosophy. But St. Augustine lays even greater emphasis on the nature of the "self" as an active will than Descartes. We recognise, accordingly, the prominent place which the doctrine of the freedom of the will holds in the earlier teaching of St. Augustine.

St. Augustine the philosopher developed into St. Augustine the theologian. He concentrated all the powers of his mind to uphold the teaching of the Church, whose authority he helped to establish securely for future centuries. His later doctrine did not conform to his earlier ideals. St. Augustine recognised that, if the Church is to be the absolute mediator between God and man, emphasis can no longer be laid on the subjective side of man's nature, or in the conception of man as enjoying free will.

St. Augustine was not prepared to deny outright the principle of free-will, but he limits its application in such a way as practically to transform it into determinism[1]. When the efforts of Augustine were chiefly directed to confute the heresy of Pelagianism, he speaks less clearly and less frequently in favour of his former doctrine of

[1] Lardner. *History of Manichees*, vol. III, 4, 13.

freedom of the will, and develops those predestinarian views, which are so well known in connection with his name.

It is not, however, true to say that he materially changed his opinions on that subject; for, in some of his most decidedly anti-Pelagian writings, whilst most strongly maintaining the sovereignty of Divine grace, he unequivocally asserts the freedom of the human will, as a gift of God to be used and accounted for.[1]

In the following pages we wish to distinguish the philosophical ideas of St. Augustine from his general system of teaching. It is quite evident that all these philosophical ideas have their ultimate ground and inner union in the principle of the immediate certainty of conscious experience. St. Augustine is the first to express this principle with complete clearness. He formulated this principle and employed it as the starting-point in the evolution of his philosophical system.

The same change, which had taken place before in the case of other philosophers, was experienced by St. Augustine. We may explain briefly the nature of this change by pointing out that, under the influence of ethical and religious tendencies, metaphysical interest has been gradually and almost imperceptibly transferred from the sphere of the outer to that of the inner life. Where introspection is carried on to a certain degree, it is natural that psychical conceptions should take the place of physical as the fundamental factors in the individual conception of the world. The same change had taken place in the views of many, both before and after the time of Augustine. This change, which had been marked in the experience of Origen and Plotinus, was brought into full and conscious use by Augustine. This ideal was

[1] *De Spiritu et Littera*, lii, also *De Lib. Arb.*

evidently present in his mind when he wrote the remarkable words: "Noli foras ire; in te ipsum redi; in interiore
homine habitat veritas".

We may regard the emphasis, which Augustine lays
upon inner experience, as that characteristic of his
teaching which constitutes the peculiar literary feature of
this great thinker. No one can deny that the Bishop of
Hippo is a virtuoso in the art of self-observation and self-
analysis. He is a master in the description of psychical
states. His skill in this respect is as admirable as his
ability to analyse psychical conditions by reflection.
Because he enjoys this faculty of introspection and self-
analysis he bases his metaphysical views of the universe
upon the most expressive principles of feeling and
impulse.

From these psychological principles of St. Augustine
begins a new system of thought, which presents a marked
contrast to that of Greek philosophy. It attracted but few
followers during the early Middle Ages.

It is remarkable that the full significance of his teaching
was not understood until a considerable time after his
death.

It is interesting to observe that when Augustine treats
of philosophical and theological problems it is from the
psychological point of view. This truth is exemplified by
his anti-Pelagian treatises, wherein his psychological
treatment of the question is of striking interest.

Augustine wrote no systematic work on the subject of
psychology. His system of thought can be discovered
from his various writings; it is eclectic, embodying
elements from Plato and the Neo-Platonists, from
Aristotle, the Peripatetics and Stoics, but the chief influence on his mind is Neo-Platonic; Augustine is,

accordingly, a thorough-going Animist in the philosophical sense of the word.

Some writers hold the opinion that Augustine's Neo-Platonic studies developed his psychological outlook, but the earlier part of his *Confessions*, written before he was influenced by Neo-Platonism, is full of accurately observed and vividly expressed inner experience. The psychology of Plotinus is, indeed, much more metaphysical than that of Augustine.

The fact is indisputable that Augustine had a natural bent for psychology. It is the basis of his thought, and provides the standpoint from which he approaches different intellectual problems. Harnack admires the African Doctor's gift of psychological introspection and his captivating facility for describing his comprehensive teaching. This gift, he says, is the secret of Augustine's originality and greatness.

Harnack also holds the opinion that Augustine was a great philosopher and psychologist because he was so great a theologian[1]. A clue to the meaning of these words can be found in the statement that Augustine made greater progress in psychology than his predecessors for the simple reason that he was a monotheist. Theological and ethical interests appear over and over again in his earlier writings. The light of eternity shines upon every part of his discourses. Even when he enters the field of discussion, God and the soul are not separated. "Deum et animam scire cupio." Augustine does not regard the soul, as Aristotle did, from a biological standpoint. For the latter, the soul was the principle of life, but Augustine regarded it rather from an ethical and religious standpoint. For Augustine, the soul is pre-eminently the

[1] Harnack. *History of Dogma*, III, p. 104.

rational element in man, and so he conceives man to be
not an animal but a rational being. The human soul is
the object not only of his scientific investigation, but also
of his love, and even in a thief, as he says, he finds the
soul lovable[1]. His treatment of the subject corresponds
very closely to the metaphysical and ethical teaching
about the soul in Plato's writings.

St. Augustine may be described as one of the most
remarkable of our ancient psychologists. It must be
remembered, however, that he is in the first place a
theologian, and in the second place a psychologist. His
influence on the history of thought and doctrine has been
so great that his opinion on any psychological subject
cannot fail to be of the greatest interest.

The Western type of thought was superior, in its
psychological aspect, to that of the East. It must be
admitted that the importance of St. Augustine's writings
in this respect has been more fully recognised in recent
years. There is considerable evidence to prove that the
interest of the English people in the psychology of the
ancients is not so great as it might be. Otto Klemm in his
Geschichte der Psychologie quotes a modern psychologist's
remark to the effect that Psychology has a long past, but
only a short history.

Great thinkers have hoped, not in vain, for better
results from the contribution of Scholasticism in the
development of modern psychology, which is largely
indebted to the teaching of St. Augustine on the subject
of behaviour. Stoic rationalism was relegated to a subordinate position by St. Augustine's all-important effort
to develop the psychology of the moral and immoral, the
pious and impious, on the basis of actual observation.

[1] *Solil.*, i, 2.

It is generally admitted that the greatness of St. Augustine as a scientific theologian is found to be essentially in his psychological principles. We may say, however, that this contribution is first discovered in the writings of Tertullian[1]. Before the time of St. Augustine, the psychological aspect of theology was not clearly expressed, for the simple reason that the principles of Eclecticism and moralism, to which the teaching of Cicero had especially given currency, prevailed widely as the result of the diffusion of his teaching which was remarkable for those times.

The language of St. Augustine is not that of a man who is exclusively a philosopher and a psychologist; there is little that is abstruse or technical in it; it is such as an ordinary man can understand. Doubtless, the reader could not fail to receive the impression that the writer had enjoyed many years of rhetorical training.

Augustine may also be described as a pioneer in the science of experimental psychology. His outlook on life affords an illustration of that concentration of interest on the individual soul, which was so characteristic of the age in which he lived. Neo-Platonism, doubtless, played its part in thus influencing him; but his moral struggle and perplexities also helped towards this end; his self-examination, his study of the Psalms and of St. Paul's Epistles also were important factors. He is filled with an overwhelming consciousness of the mystery of his own being; above all, the crowning enigma—the portent ("monstrum"), the disease ("ægritudo") of the divided will[2]. He is fascinated especially by the complicated problems connected with the faculty of memory—that

[1] See Tertullian's great writing, De Anima.
[2] Sol., i, 8–9, 21.

unfathomable treasury of thought and perception. "Great," he cries, "is the power of memory, inconceivably marvellous, O my God, profound and infinite in its manifoldness! And this thing is the mind, and I myself am it. What then am I, O my God? What is my nature? A life various, multiform, and of exceeding vastness".[1]

Augustine was no ordinary psychologist. He may be described as a man of deep constructive thoughts. Not only was he versed in all the psychological learning of his day, which was more than most people would imagine, but he ranks also as a pioneer in the practice of accurate observation. He had bestowed much attention on the larger problems which confront the psychologist "in limine," the origin of the individual soul and the exact nature of its relation to the body; declining to accept any easy solution, he felt compelled to conclude, like so many honest thinkers before and since, that certain problems must be left unsolved. He had a superficial knowledge of the working of the nervous system, and for information, he consulted, as he tells us, not the philosophers, but the physicians. His treatment of the subject of memory evokes the admiration of historians of psychology; he distinguishes clearly between intuitive and ratiocinative intellection, and he even refers to the relation of the conscious to the sub-conscious mind. His skill in introspection is clearly evident on almost every page of the *Confessions*; but it is more remarkable to find him showing an intelligent interest in what we to-day describe as the "modern" studies of crowd-psychology and child psychology.

It is important to remember the adequacy of his psychological equipment, since this factor furnishes both

[1] *Sol.*, i, 10, 17, 26.

to his personal observations of psychic phenomena and to his criticism of the statements of others a much greater value than they would otherwise have.

Modern psychology has rightly adopted the traditions of St. Augustine and Leibniz. The conception of psychological latency has now become of such fundamental importance that it serves to explain all psychic activity. Every psychologist can now recognise such mental operations as "implicit" representations, "mediated" association, the formation of representative and conceptual groupings, intuition, and so forth. Several writers (e.g. Ach. Marbe, Bühler, and others) have demonstrated in the clearest possible manner the importance of unconscious processes in the formation of concepts, conclusions, and determinations.

In conclusion, we may add that Augustine has accomplished for Christian psychology what Athanasius did for Christian metaphysics; and as it is on psychological questions that he has shed most light, we are naturally inclined to consider him chiefly from that point of view, not forgetting, of course, the part he played in the theological disputes of his day.

Chapter I

INFLUENCE OF ANCIENT WRITERS

Africa was the birthplace of the poet Nemesianus, Tertullian, Minucius Felix, Cyprian, Arnobius and Lactantius.

Since the end of the reign of Marcus Aurelius, the schools of the Romanised Carthaginians had developed in a remarkable manner. Carthage, rebuilt under Augustus (29 B.C.), had become celebrated for its masters and studies. "Carthage," exclaimed Apuleius, "is the venerable instructor of our whole province. Carthage is the heavenly muse of Africa—the inspirer of the Roman people!"[1]

Passing from Carthage to Rome, and thence to Milan, St. Augustine was influenced by the intellectual culture of these places.

His numerous quotations from, and references to, ancient philosophers and thinkers enable us to understand how great was their influence on the mind of St. Augustine.

St. Augustine is described by Gennadius as "Vir acer ingenio, in divinis scripturis doctus, Graeca et Latina lingua scholasticus."[2]

On the one hand, St. Augustine is not a stranger to any of the doctrines of his time. On the other hand, he is the accredited representative, the unconquerable and convincing defender of Christianity and the Church.

A study of the pages of St. Augustine's writings will

[1] Apuleius *Florides*, IV, 21.
[2] *Script. Eccl.*, 46.

22

enable the student to recognise numerous evidences of
proper names, of allusions, and of reminiscences.
Anagoras and Anaximander, Anaximenes and Antis-
thenes, Aristotle and Carneades, Epicletus and Epicurus,
Pythagoras and Zenocrates, Plato and Plotinus, Porphyry
and Iamblichus, Apollonius and Apuleius, Cicero and
Seneca, Horace and Vergil, Perseus and Terence,
Bardesanes and Manes, St. Paul and St. Ambrose,
Tertullian and Athanasius, Greeks and Latins, Philosophers and Poets. He refers to the most illustrious
persons of antiquity, both sacred and profane.

In the eighth book of the *De Civitate Dei*, St. Augustine
mentions that he was no stranger to ancient philosophy[1].
"Plato," he says, "has enabled me to know the true God;
Jesus Christ has revealed the vision to me."[2]

There can be no doubt that St. Augustine derived the
basic principles of natural theology from Plato—his conception of God is that He is an incorporeal light. The
proof which he gives of the Spirituality of the soul is
altogether Platonic. St. Augustine, indeed, borrowed
largely from the system of Plato.

If we employ modern terminology, we may say that
the teaching of Plato suggested to Augustine the two-fold
aspect of things—the subjective and the objective—
which we may describe as the psychological and the
ontological outlook. He adopted the subjective and
psychological aspect of the Platonic theory of ideas. This
teaching influenced his ideas of God, Creation, the Logos,
and his teaching generally. The pages of the *Timaeus*
clearly reveal the numerous similarities between the
statements of Plato and of St. Augustine. This influence

[1] *De Civ. Dei*, viii, 2.
[2] *Cf. Cont. Jul. Pelag.*, iv, 14.

is evident in the *Confessions*, the *De Civitate Dei* and his other writings.

St. Augustine's Christian conception of the World became intelligible as the result of his education. Every stage in his career appears to have influenced him. His pagan father and pious Christian mother, Cicero's *Hortensius*, Manichaeism, Aristotelianism, Neo-Platonism, with its mysticism and scepticism, the impression produced by Ambrose and Monachism, all contributed their share[1].

It is evident that Augustine was also familiar with the philosophical writings of Apuleius. When it is remembered that Augustine was sent for the purpose of study to Madura, the birthplace of Lucius Apuleius, it is natural to believe that Augustine would learn to admire the works of one whom his father and all his teachers had regarded as a model. In fact, Augustine often alludes to Apuleius in his *De Civitate Dei*, citing him as an example in demonstrating the importance of the art of magic. In fact, Apuleius appears to have been the first writer to make an impression on the mind of Augustine and to urge him to engage in the study of philosophy and especially of Cicero's *Hortensius*, for the purpose of concentrating his reflective powers upon the divine mysteries. The writings of Apuleius left the mark of their influence on the mind of Augustine at the time when he was desirous of pursuing his studies. Apuleius and Augustine were lovers of beautiful speech and subtlety of thought; both may be described as mystics. Augustine's love for astrology in his later years may have been the result of his admiration for this dabbler in magic.

At one time Augustine was a worshipper of style for

[1] See Essay by G. Boissier in the *Rev. de deux mondes*, January, 1888.

its own sake. The atmosphere of mystery which pervades the works of Apuleius doubtless helped to awaken the spirit of religion in Augustine and influenced him to study the mysterious aspect of Christianity.

The sources to which Augustine turned for information were Greek and Latin, and this was quite natural. He enjoyed a remarkable knowledge of Plato's *Timaeus*, and adopted his theory of ideas. But the Platonism upon which he drew was the Alexandrian Neo-Platonism of Plotinus, Porphyry and Iamblichus; he relied on the translation of the rhetorician Victorinus, and not on the original documents. His unsatisfactory knowledge of Greek, and his study of the teaching of Plato in the Neo-Platonic writings above mentioned, influenced him to classify the treatises of Plato and Aristotle, Academicians and Peripatetics, Platonists and Neo-Platonists as constituting one system, without the least suspicion of their divergent points of view.

His knowledge of the Greek Fathers was acquired through the Antiochian school, whose methods, views, and arguments respecting the explanation of the Trinity, he repeats with a remarkable similarity as is indicative of the fusion of Greek and Latin thought-currents.[1]

In addition to his knowledge of Hellenic science, Augustine was greatly indebted to Latin writers for much of his knowledge. At Carthage, Augustine became very familiar with the whole range of Latin literature. Aspiring to be a teacher of rhetoric he studied carefully the speeches of Cicero. He learned apt quotations from the Odes and Satires of Horace. He acquired a knowledge of the writings of Terence, Lucretius, Persius, Juvenal, and Seneca, and from all of them he quotes in the *Confessions*.

[1] *Dict. of Phil. and Psy.*, vol. II, p. 273.

He appreciated Sallust especially for his careful choice of appropriate expressions, "lectissimus pensator verborum."[1] His favourite Latin author was Vergil, of whom he writes: "This most famous and approved of all poets." He strongly commended the practice of teaching his verses to the young. Augustine quotes lines from Vergil in his letters and theological treatises.[2] Of the Latin Fathers, Tertullian, Lactantius, and Ambrose, were most useful to him.

A great amount of very important knowledge was received from the East and preserved for the West by Greek scholars, especially Hilary, Ambrose, and Jerome. at a time when the influence of Greek writers was not so powerful as it had been in the West. In the philosophical, historical, and theological elements of Greek thought, transplanted by them, we find one of the formative influences at work on the mind of St. Augustine.

He learned the science of exegetical study and explanation from Ambrose, the disciple of the Cappadocians, and it was only by means of it that he was completely delivered from Manichaeism. He acquired a remarkable knowledge of the ideals of the Egyptian monks and the impression, thus received, exercised a great influence on him.

Although Augustine's reading was carried on from a literary and rhetorical point of view, yet he found time to study philosophy. He refers in his treatises to the most distinguished writers of Greece and Rome. In the course of his study of the writings of Cicero, he came across the Dialogue, which has been lost, entitled *Hortensius*, or *De Philosophia*, to which he refers in *Conf.* vii 17.

[1] *De Beata Vita*, 31.
[2] Combés. *St. Augustine et la culture Classique*, p. 19.

Several fragments, however, of this lost work have been preserved, some by Augustine himself, some by Lactantius, Nonius, and others. There is no reason to doubt that this Dialogue contained an eloquent plea for the study of philosophy. It made a deep impression on the mind of Augustine, changed his outlook, turned the current of his thoughts Godward, and awakened a great intellectual hunger for abstract truth. It incited him to engage in additional philosophical studies and awakened in him new ideas and interests. How deep was the impression made upon him may be inferred from the high terms he employs in practising it in his *Confessions*; although he had studied it twenty-six years previously, he quotes from it on more than one occasion in his later writings, e.g. in *De Civitate Dei*, in *De Trinitate*, and in his reply to Julian the Pelagian advocate. He appears, however, to be disappointed with the treatise in one respect, namely, the absence of Christ's name "that blessed name which his childish heart had sucked in with his mother's milk." He adds these words "Whatever is without that name—cultivated, polished and true as it may be—did not take complete hold of me."[1] Another passage in the work now lost, which impressed Augustine, is quoted in *De Trin.*, xiv 26: "If, as was thought by ancient philosophers and by those much the greatest and most famous, we have souls that are eternal and akin to the divine, we must believe that the more these devote themselves to their proper course—that is, to the cultivation of reason and the desire of investigation—and the less they become involved in the errors and vices of mankind, so much the more easy do they experience the ascent (of the soul) and its return to heaven."

[1] *Conf.*, iii, 8.

His great love of philosophical study incited Augustine to further intellectual pursuits. Cicero's enthusiasm inspired his reader. The study of *Hortensius* opened up another world of study to the young scholar. In this way he became conscious of his latent mental power for speculative thought. His other studies became subordinate to his search for truth. Instead of adopting the profession of a teacher of rhetoric, as his parents desired, he directed his attention to the study of the Roman form of Greek thought.

From *Conf.*, iii, 7, we learn that it was his study of the *Hortensius* which excited his enthusiasm for the things of the mind and consequently caused him to form a lower estimate of the importance of wealth and worldly success.

The chief result of his study of this lost work, however, was that Augustine was impelled to turn to consult the Scriptures, hoping in them to discover the path of wisdom, which he was now most desirous of following. Cicero's treatise awakened a responsive echo in his mind, but it left his religious instinct unsatisfied. It failed to impart the great secret of self-mastery. Where spiritual wisdom was to be found, the *Hortensius* was silent. Augustine was, accordingly, left without any religious principles or standards of truth to support him.

Augustine became acquainted with the *Categories* of Aristotle when he was barely twenty years of age, as Plotinus and Porphyry had done before him. He tells us that he considered Aristotle to be "a man of outstanding ability and eloquence, but not equal to Plato." He studied the *Categories*, independently of the assistance of any teacher, and understood them. "With restless impatience I earnestly desired to understand this treatise, a thing sublime and divine. I read and understood it without help. I found others who had studied it with great difficulty, with the assistance of masters and diagrams, and they understood it no better than I did."[1] Porphyry's *Introduction to the Categories* is still extant.[2] So great, indeed, was the influence of the writings of Aristotle on the mind of Augustine, that Julian of Eclanum is said to have applied the decisive title "Aristoteles Poenorum" to Augustine.[3]

About the beginning of the year A.D. 386, Augustine had the good fortune to come across certain Platonic and Neo-Platonic writings, which had been translated into Latin by the rhetorician Victorinus—an "Augustinian before Augustine" as he has been termed. His conversion to Christianity is the subject of a well-known part of Augustine's *Confessions* (viii, 2–5). Augustine regarded him as his model, in certain respects, at a very critical epoch in his career. When Victorinus became a Christian, he did not abandon Neo-Platonism. He was a very ardent follower of St. Paul and devoted to the Apostle's teaching of the doctrine of justification by faith. His language, certainly, is decidedly anti-Pelagian. Although Augustine knew a sufficient amount of Greek to read the Neo-Platonic writings, yet it was by Victorinus that he was instructed about them. The *Perihermenias* and *Topica* appeared in translations by Victorinus.

Augustine carefully studied this philosophy by consulting treatises which were well known to him, and he tells us that they awakened his zeal.[4] This knowledge

---

[1] *Conf.*, iv, 16, 28.
[2] See Ueberweg, *Hist. of Philosophy*, i, 251.
[3] Aug. *Op. imperf.*, iii, 199.
[4] *Cont. Acad.*, ii, 5.

completely delivered him from the bondage of Manichaean dualism and Academic scepticism, and caused him to turn his thoughts inwards and upwards. Carried away by his enthusiasm, he believed that he had already discovered the hitherto hidden sources of wisdom. He soon learned, however, that it is not the abstract knowledge of the truth, but the fact of being influenced by it, which alone could bring peace to his soul.[1]

Bishop Gore says of Victorinus[2]: "It is worth while calling attention to the evidence, suggested by a good deal of Victorinus's theology, of a closer connection than has been yet noticed between him and St. Augustine. His strong insistence in his Trinitarian theology on the double Procession of the Holy Spirit—his conception of the Holy Spirit as the 'Bond' of the Blessed Trinity; his emphasis on the unity of Christ and His Church; his strong predestinarianism; his vehement assertion of the doctrine of grace; his assertion of the priority of faith to intelligence; all reappear in St. Augustine, and it may be that the (hitherto unsuspected) influence of the writings of the old philosopher whose conversion stirred him so deeply was a determining force upon the theology of St. Augustine."

Stoicism, naturally, influenced the mind of St. Augustine, but Stoic rationalism was relegated to a secondary position by his supreme effort to establish the psychology of the moral and the immoral, the pious and the impious on the basis of actual observation. His greatness as a "scientific" thinker consists essentially in his appeal to psychological principles. St. Augustine's attitude to the popular philosophy of Christian Stoicism

---

[1] P. Schaff. *St. Augustine, Melancthon, Neander*, p. 50.
[2] Art. "Victorinus," *Dict. of Ch. Biog.*

of Western teachers was an important factor in his spiritual development.

The influence of the teaching of Plotinus, the noblest representative of Greek philosophy, on both the East and the West has been remarkable. Victorinus translated many of his books into Latin and one of these was probably the *Enneads*, which is thought to have been one of the "Canonical Scriptures" of the Neo-Platonists.[1] There are many passages in the writings of Plotinus which exhibit a remarkable parallelism to statements in the *Confessions* of St. Augustine. In their manner of life and in their mode of thinking they had much in common. Augustine was told by a friend that some statements often sounded like the echoes of passages in the writings of Plotinus.[2]

Dean Inge remarks that Plotinus, read in a Latin translation, was the schoolmaster who brought Augustine to Christ. There is, therefore, nothing startling in the considered opinion of Rudolf Eucken, that Plotinus has influenced Christian theology more than any other thinker (since St. Paul he should, no doubt, have added).[3]

Speaking of the influence of Neo-Platonism on the mind of St. Augustine, Grandgeorge says: "We ought to admit, first of all, that Neo-Platonism contributed powerfully in forming the mind of St. Augustine: but the reading of his works will convince us that this fact, far from being a constant quantity, has a tendency to become less marked."[4]

Grandgeorge mentions that St. Augustine was

---

[1] *Conf.*, viii, 2. *Cont. Acad.*, iii, 18, 41.
[2] *Ep.* vi: "illæ mihi Christum, illæ Platonem, illæ Plotinum sonabunt."
[3] W. R. Inge. *The Philosophy of Plotinus*, vol. I, p. 12.
[4] Grandgeorge. *St. Augustin et Le Néo-Platonisme*, p. 3.

acquainted with each of the six *Enneads* of Plotinus, and that he quotes him by name five times. Augustine speaks of him in the following terms: "The teaching of Plato, the most pure and bright in all philosophy, driving away the clouds of error, shines forth most of all in Plotinus, the Platonic philosopher who has been regarded as so like his master that we might think of them as contemporaries, if the time which has elapsed between them did not compel us merely to say that in Plotinus Plato lived again."[1] In his later writings, Augustine refers to the "very acute and able men" who were scholars in the school of Plotinus at Rome; he regrets that some of them were led astray by curious arts, and thinks that, if Plotinus and his friends had lived a little later, they would have "changed a few words and phrases and become Christians, as many of the Platonists in our generation have done.[2]

St. Augustine accurately reproduces in his treatise *De Immortalitate Animae*, viii, the argument of Plotinus about the soul's being an uncompounded substance.

It is not difficult to appreciate at its true value the influence of Neo-Platonism upon the mind of the great African saint. It is not likely that anyone, who has carefully studied the writings of St. Augustine, will deny this influence; it is sufficient for anyone who doubts this statement to read carefully those passages from the writings of Plotinus and Augustine which have been arranged in parallel columns by M. Grandgeorge.[3]

The same writer also observes that so long as his philosophy is in agreement with his religious doctrines, "St. Augustine is frankly Neo-Platonist; as soon as a

[1] *Cont. Acad.*, iii, 18.
[2] *Ep.* 118. *De Vera Relig.*, 12.
[3] *St. Augustin et le Néo-Platonisme*, p. 117–147.

difference arises, he never hesitates to subordinate his philosophy to religion, and his reason to faith."[1] There can be no doubt, however, that he thought that it would be an easy task to find Christianity in Plato, and Platonism in the Gospel.

There is no reason to doubt that Neo-Platonism influenced the West, at first only through the medium or under the cloak of Christian theology. We can believe that even Boethius was a Catholic Christian. In his mode of thought he was certainly a Neo-Platonist. "In antiquity itself," says Harnack, "Neo-Platonism influenced, with special directness, one Western theologian, and that the most important, viz. Augustine."

In the seventh book of his *Confessions* he acknowledges his indebtedness to the Neo-Platonic writings. In reference to the most important doctrines, about God, matter, the relation of God to the world, freedom and evil, Augustine is always dependent on the teaching of Neo-Platonism; but, at the same time, it must be admitted that, of all theologians of antiquity, he was the one who recognised most clearly and declared most plainly wherein Christianity and Neo-Platonism differ.[2]

Harnack asserts that St. Augustine was both positively and negatively influenced by Neo-Platonism, as represented by the teaching of Plotinus and Porphyry; negatively, in so far as he found in this teaching a doctrine of the Trinity—a doctrine which was based on a descending series of emanations; positively, in so far as he derived from Plotinus the idea of the simplicity of God, and attempted to make use of it. To St. Augustine, as a philosopher, the development of a doctrine of the

[1] Ibid, 155.
[2] *Hist. of Dogma*, I, p. 361.

C

Trinity was already a matter of course.[1] The Augustinian interpretation regards the Persons of the Trinity as conceptions, and leaves but little room for the expression of ordinary or pictorial thought.

St. Augustine gave the stamp of absolute conviction to what before had been uncertain, viz. that God operates continuously by a mysterious and omnipotent gift of grace, i.e. by powers of grace. When we study carefully the seventh and eighth Books of the *Confessions*, and also the writings composed immediately after his conversion, we discover that his Neo-Platonism undoubtedly contributed to this belief. But he was influenced to a greater degree by his inner experience, and by the reading of the Psalms and of St. Paul's Epistles. His earlier writings, indeed, were more Neo-Platonic than those of his later life.

St. Augustine prefers to concentrate his attention on the writings of the later Platonists, "qui Platonem ceteris philosophis gentium longe recteque praelatum acutius atque veracius intellexisse atque secute esse fama celebriore laudantur." He numbers Aristotle among the Old Platonists, and adds that he founded a "secta" or "haeresis" of his own, distinct from that of the Academics; he describes him as a "vir excellentis ingenii et eloquio Platoni quidem impar, sed multos facile superans."[2]

The later followers of Plato desired to be called neither Academics nor Peripatetics, but Platonists, pre-eminent among whom were Plotinus, Porphyry, and Iamblichus. For them God is the "causa subsistendi," the "ratio intelligendi," and the "ordo vivendi."[3] "No philosophers," says St. Augustine, "have approached nearer

---

[1] *Hist. of Dogma*, IV, p. 132.
[2] *De Civ. Dei*, viii, 12.
[3] *De Civ. Dei*, iv.

to us than they." (Ch. V). Their doctrine is superior to the "fabulous religion" of the poets, the "civil religion" of the pagan state, and the "natural religion" of all ancient philosophers, including that of the Stoics, who believed they could find the first cause of all things in fire, and that of the Epicureans, who found the cause in atoms; both these sects of philosophy were too sensualistic in their theories of knowledge and too little theological in their ethics. In their search for the eternal and immutable God, the Platonists, with reason, passed beyond the material world, the soul, and the realm of mutable spirits.[1]

But they were unwilling to accept the truth as held by Christians. They paid religious veneration not only to the supreme God but also to inferior deities and demons, who are not creators.[2] The Christian, even without the aid of philosophy, knows from the teaching of the Holy Scriptures that God is our Creator, our teacher, and the giver of grace.[3]

The influence of Aristotle is evident in St. Augustine's picture of the progress of the individual soul to God.[4] All life is a development, and St. Augustine distinguishes seven stages (stadia) in this progress. Defining these stadia, he adopts the Aristotelian doctrine as his guide, but (following the analogy of the Neo-Platonic doctrine of the higher virtues) he goes further than that doctrine leads him. The stadia are marked by (1) the vegetative forces; (2) the animal forces (including memory and imagination); (3) the rational force, on which the development of the arts and sciences depends; (4) virtue, as the purification of the soul attained by struggling against sensual

[1] De Civ. Dei, viii, 6.
[2] De Civ. Dei, xii, 24.
[3] De Civ. Dei, viii, 10.
[4] De Quant. Anim., 72 ff.

pleasure and by faith in God; (5) security in goodness; (6) attaining unto God; (7) the eternal vision of God. By attaining to the vision of God we arrive at complete likeness to God, whereby we do not indeed become God, nor like God Himself, but His image is restored in us.[1]

Although we are compelled to recognise the influence of Greek philosophy, yet we find that, at times, he starts off on an independent line of thought which is quite original, derived from an entirely different source.

Much of the Dualism, which we find expressed in *De Civitate Dei*, appears to owe its origin to the writings of Tyconius, a Donatist writer of the fourth century. Tyconius can be better described as an "Afro-Catholic," as he did not believe that the Donatists were exclusively the only true Church, but that they formed part of the Catholic Church, although not in communion with it. Tyconius owes nothing to classical culture or to philosophical ideas; his inspiration is entirely Biblical and Hebraic. Thus it appears that Augustine was able to appreciate the obscure and tortuous originality of Tyconius as well as the clear classicism of Cicero.

In *De Doctrina Christiana* Augustine incorporates the *Rules* of Tyconius. Augustine was also influenced by him in his interpretation of Scripture, in his theology, and in his outlook on history. In two of his treatises, *On Catechising the unlearned*, and in *The City of God*, Augustine takes up the idea of Tyconius in his commentary on the Apocalypse. "Behold two Cities, the City of God and the City of the Devil. . . . One of them desires to serve the world, the other to fly from this world. One is afflicted, and the other rejoices; one smites, and the other is smitten; one slays, and the other is slain;

---

[1] *De Trin.*, xiii, 12; xiv, 24.

the one in order to be the more justified thereby, the other to fill up the measure of its iniquities. And each of them strives together, the one that it may receive damnation, the other that it may attain salvation."[1]

Another writer who influenced Augustine was Varro, whose *Book of Antiquities* was, doubtless, familiar to the writer of *De Civitate Dei*, where, in the last twelve chapters, evidence of its use is apparent. This work has been lost, but it appears to have been a complete mythology of Italy, minutely describing everything relating to religious ceremonial.

Harnack describes the nature of the influence which the writers of the past exercised on the mind of St. Augustine. Referring to the influence of Ambrose, he says: "We cannot appreciate too highly the important influence exerted on after times, and first on Augustine, by Ambrose's expression of his personal religion. The light that dawned in Augustine's *Confessions* already shone from the works of Ambrose, and it was the latter, not the former, who conducted Western piety to the specific love of Christ."[2]

It must be admitted, however, that, after Augustine's complete conversion to Catholic Christianity, his Platonism continued to be ineradicable, and he used the thoughts and language of Plato's philosophy, interpreted by the Neo-Platonic School, as the vehicle for the development and expression of Christian truth and theology, just as naturally and as whole-heartedly as St. Thomas Aquinas relied on those of Aristotle.[3]

---

[1] Beatus. *Comm. in Apoc.*, ed. Florex, p. 506–7.
[2] *Hist. of Dogma*, III, p. 30.
[3] Dom. C. Butler. *Western Mysticism*, p. 87.

CHAPTER II

THE INFLUENCE OF THE TEACHING OF ST. PAUL ON THE DOCTRINE AND TERMINOLOGY OF ST. AUGUSTINE

ST. AUGUSTINE was deeply influenced by the study of the Epistles of St. Paul, and read them through collectively with the greatest care and admiration. Here he found all those truths, which addressed him in Platonism, no longer obscurely foreshadowed, but fulfilled; and yet much more besides.[1] Here he found Christ as the Mediator between God and man, between heaven and earth, Who alone can give us power to attain those lofty ideals and embody them in life. It is especially important to remember that here he read that masterly delineation of the conflict between the spirit and the flesh,[2] which was literally confirmed by his own experience. Here he learned to know aright the depth of the ruin and the utter impossibility of being delivered from it by any natural wisdom or natural strength, and, at the same time, the great remedy, which God graciously offers to us in His Beloved Son.[3]

We may, indeed, describe the teaching of St. Augustine as a Paulinism modified by popular Catholic elements.

"I have undertaken, O my God," says St. Augustine, "to read with eagerness Your Sacred Writings, inspired by the Holy Spirit, and especially the Epistles of the Apostle Paul. I have begun to recognise that all that I have read in the book of philosophers, I have

[1] *Confess.*, vii, 21.
[2] *Rom.*, vii.
[3] P. Schaff. *St. Augustin, Melancthon, Neander,* 52 f.

found it in Your Scriptures, with the help of Thy Grace."[1]

Harnack asserts that the direct influence of the writings of St. Paul was supplemented by the teaching of Victorinus, "Unless all signs deceive," he says, "Augustine received from Victorinus the impulse which led him to assimilate Paul's type of religious thought; for it appears from the works of the aged rhetorician that he had appropriated Paul's characteristic ideas, and Augustine demonstrably devoted a patient study to the Pauline epistles from the moment when he became more thoroughly acquainted with Neo-Platonism."[2]

The Paulinism of the Alexandrines is an important factor in the development of thought. We appreciate their contribution to religion, to the grasp of opinion upon conduct. They endeavoured to show that Christianity is not a doctrine but a life, not a law but a spirit. The Christian must be holy yet free, obedient yet intelligent, able to judge and act for himself, a true son of God, needing no earthly director, because guided by his Father's eye.

St. Augustine's intense study of the writings of St. Paul and the Psalms began after he had broken with Manichaeism and had been convinced by Neo-Platonism that God was a spiritual substance (spiritalis substantia). Even the expositions in the earliest writings, which are apparently purely philosophical, were already dominated by the Christian conviction that God, the world, and the Ego were to be distinguished, and that room was to be made for the distinction in mystical speculation.

Anyone who disregards the formulae, and looks

[1] *Confessions*, vii, 21.
[2] *Hist. of Dogma*, V, p. 34.

rather to the spirit of his teaching, will everywhere find in St. Augustine's works a stream of Pauline faith.

Numerous passages can be cited, in which St. Augustine extolled faith as the element in which the soul lives, as the beginning, middle, and end of piety. And yet, after all, it was not in faith, but only in love, that he could recognise the force that really changed a man's nature, that set him in a new relationship.

We are justified in asserting that St. Augustine held that the relation of the pious soul to God may be most appropriately described as a gradually advancing process of sanctification.

We cannot, indeed, understand St. Augustine as teacher of the Church, until we have formed our estimate of him as a reformer of piety; for, besides Scripture and tradition, his theories have their strongest roots in the piety that animated him. They are in part nothing but states of feeling interpreted theoretically. But in these states of feeling there gathered round the grand experience of conversion from bondage to freedom in God all the manifold religious experiences and moral reflections of the ancient world. The Psalms and Paul, Plato and the Neo-Platonists, the Moralists, Tertullian and Ambrose, we find all again in Augustine, and, side by side with the new psychological view constructed by him as disciple of the Neo-Platonists, we come once more upon all the childish reflections and absolute theories which these men had pursued.[1]

It is evident that in the writings of St. Paul and those allied to him, the Greek expressions for the intellectual elements in man have acquired an important place, although they are not stated with very marked precision.

[1] Harnack. *Hist. of Dogma*, V, p. 94

St. Paul, especially, has a firm conception of Mind (Nous) as the highest expression for man's mental or intellectual faculty, as that which in man, under grace, is appealed to by the Divine law.[1] and as that, on the other hand, which is to be distinguished from the "afflatus" or influence of the supernatural upon him.[2]

Then there is introduced into these writings a free use of the similar and related terms, in which the Greek language was so rich—understanding σύνεσις, reason λόγος, reasoning διαλογισμός, thinkings νοήματα, minding or disposition φρόνημα, but scarcely any one of these is used with strictness or accuracy.

St. Paul says: "I had not known lust except the law had said 'Thou shalt not covet'." The psychological truth here suggested exercised a great influence on the mind of St. Augustine.

St. Augustine falsely applies the words of St. Paul: "Whatsoever is not of faith, is sin,"[3] for he ascribed all the virtues of the heathen to ambition and love of honour, and accordingly stigmatises them as vices.[4] And, in fact, he is in this respect inconsistent with himself. For, according to his view, the nature which God created remains as to its substance, good; the divine image is not wholly lost, but only defaced; and even man's sorrow in his loss reveals a remaining trace of good.[5]

In many respects the influence of St. Paul is evident.

St. Paul's doctrine of human nature is that of the Old Testament. Man is constituted of flesh and spirit. By the

---

[1] *Rom.* vii, 23, 25.
[2] I *Cor.* xiv, 14, 15.
[3] *Rom.* xiv, 23.
[4] *De Civ. Dei* v, 13–20; xix, 25.
[5] *De Genesi ad lit.*, viii, 14; *Retract.*, ii, 24.

former he is allied to the perishable material, by the latter
to God and the unseen world. The "soul" with St. Paul,
as throughout the Scripture, is not a "tertium quid" between the flesh and the spirit; it is rather their unity, the
living self behind the bodily form of each man.

The word "soul" is but seldom employed by St. Paul.
He employs the term "heart," as the seat of the manifold
thoughts and feelings, instead. The "soul" ($\psi v \chi \acute{\eta}$) concentrates the thoughts and the feelings into the self, the
conscious Ego. Three terms must especially be distin-
guished: "spirit" ($\pi v \varepsilon \tilde{v} \mu a$) is the principle, "soul"
($\psi v \chi \acute{\eta}$) the subject, and "heart" ($\varkappa a \varrho \delta \acute{\iota} a$)the organ of life.

"Spirit" ($\pi v \varepsilon \tilde{v} \mu a$), as a faculty of knowledge, when
directed towards Divine things is called $v o \tilde{v} \varsigma$ in the
Epistle to the Romans i, 20, vii, 23–25, etc.; the same
power introverted is the ethical self-consciousness called
"conscience" ($\sigma v v \acute{\varepsilon} \iota \delta \eta \sigma \iota \varsigma$) in Romans ii, 15, etc.

Lightfoot speaks in somewhat strong terms of the
word "conscience" as the "crowning triumph of ethical
nomenclature" which, "if not struck in the mint of the
Stoics, at all events became current coin through their
influence." He cites it as a special instance of "the extent
to which Stoic philosophy had leavened the moral
vocabulary of the civilised world at the time of the
Christian era."

Its use in the New Testament precisely corresponds to
this estimate. It occurs twice in the addresses of St. Paul
recorded in Acts and several times in his Epistles. In all
these passages its force is equivalent to that which it still
bears in modern speech. St. John uses the term "heart"
($\varkappa a \varrho \delta \acute{\iota} a$)[1] in a connection where St. Paul would have
used "mind" ($v o \tilde{v} \varsigma$) or "conscience" ($\sigma v v \acute{\varepsilon} \iota \delta \eta \sigma \iota \varsigma$).

[1] I Jno. iii, 19–21.

In the Epistles of St. Paul the terms "flesh" and "Spirit" are employed in a more specific religious sense, which is based upon, but distinguishable from, their psychological meaning. The former term is always employed to denote *the sinful nature of man*. The term "spirit," on the other hand, indicates *the influence of God*, which operates in and through His spirit.[1]

The question naturally arises whether the Apostle referred sin to the constitution of man, and regarded it as the result of his physical system, and as intrinsic to matter.

The influence of the teaching and terminology of St. Paul on St. Augustine is evident.

St. Augustine appealed chiefly and repeatedly to the words in Romans (v, 12) "by which all have sinned" (ἐφ' ᾧ πάντες ἥμαρτον), which are erroneously translated by the Vulgate; "in quo omnes peccaverunt."[2]

As St. Augustine had but slight knowledge of Greek, he commonly confined himself to the Latin Bible, and here he referred the "in quo" to Adam (the "one man" in the beginning of the verse, which is far too remote); but the Greek in the above sentence (ἐφ' ᾧ) must be taken as neuter and as a conjunction in the sense, *on the ground that*, or *because*, all have sinned. The exegesis of St. Augustine and his doctrine of a *personal* fall, as it were, of all men in Adam, are therefore doubtless untenable.

On the other hand, St. Paul unquestionably teaches in this passage a casual connection between sin and death, and also a casual connection between the sin of Adam and the sinfulness of his posterity, therefore original sin. The proof of this is found in the whole parallel between Adam

[1] E.g. *Rom.* viii, 1–17. *Gal.* v, 16–25.
[2] Cf. *De peccat. merit. et remissione*, I, 8, 10; *Op. imperf.* II, 63.

and Christ, and their representative relation to mankind,[1] and especially in the phrase "all have sinned" παντες ἥμαρτον, (but not in the term ἐφ᾽ ᾧ) as translated by the Vulgate and St. Augustine. Other passages of Scripture to which St. Augustine appealed, as teaching original sin, were such as Gen. viii, 21, Ps. li, 7, St. John iii, 6, I Cor. vii, 14, Eph. ii, 3.

The contrast, drawn by St. Paul, between Jew and Christian leads him to refer to himself in a striking autobiographical passage,[2] which, though brief, may be compared for spirit and tone to St. Augustine's *Confessions*.

In *De Fide et Operibus* St. Augustine points out that St. Paul pressed his doctrine of justification so far as to be in peril of being misunderstood.[3]

In his work *The Morals of the Catholic Church*, St. Augustine quotes, for the first time, the Pauline doctrine of grace, which became, at a later time, one of the most characteristic ruling principles of his teaching; "The love of God is shed abroad in our hearts by the Holy Spirit which is given unto us."[4]

St. Paul's aspiration in the prayer for supernatural strength is expressed in *De Musica*: "O wretched man that I am, who shall deliver me from the body of this death?" St. Augustine, also, quotes the answer: "The Grace of God through Jesus Christ Our Lord."

The classical passage quoted in the story of Augustine's conversion: "Not in rioting and drunkenness, not in

---

[1] *Cf.* I *Cor.* xv, 4, 5 ff.
[2] *Phil.* iii, 4–9.
[3] xiv, 21.
[4] *Rom.* v, 5.

chambering and wantonness, not in strife and envying; but put ye on the Lord Jesus Christ and make not provision for the flesh to fulfil the lusts thereof,"[1] clearly demonstrates the reverence and importance Augustine attached to St. Paul's words.

One special passage from St. Paul's Epistles appears to make a great impression on the mind of Augustine: "For the invisible things of Him from the creation of the World are clearly seen, being understood by the things that are made, even his eternal power and Godhead; so that they are without excuse."[2] Augustine refers to this passage in his *Confessions* on more than one occasion, e.g. vii, 10, 17, bis; 20 x 6, bis; xiii 21.

Augustine's idea of grace, as described in the *Confessions* is similar to that of St. Paul in Eph. i, 7, in reference to the fact that forgiveness overcomes sin. Augustine writes: "I ascribe it to Thy grace and to Thy mercy that Thou hast dissolved my sins like the ice."[3]

It is not too much to say that the Christology of the *Confessions* is of the distinctly Pauline type; it is embodied in certain antithetic phrases as "Dominum Jesum . . . humilem"; "infirma Divinitas"; "in quantum homo, in tantum mediator; in quantum verbum, non medius, quia aequalis Deo et Deus apud Deum."[4] As St. Paul exclaims: "He loved me and gave Himself for me"; so Augustine says: "He, Thine Only One, in Whom are hid all the treasures of wisdom and knowledge, redeemed me by His blood."

[1] *Rom.* xiii, 13, 14.
[2] *Rom.* i, 20.
[3] *Conf.*, ii, 7.
[4] *Conf.*, vii, 18, 24; x, 43, 68, 70.

Some scholars think that Ambrose and Augustine together inaugurated a Pauline revival in religious thought. Certainly the conceptions of sin and redemption, grace and freedom, to which these Western teachers give systematic form and wider currency are clearly based on the express teaching of St. Paul.

CHAPTER III

INFLUENCE OF MANICHAEISM

(i) The doctrine of Man

In treating of the subject of the influence of Manichaeism on the mind of St. Augustine, it is important to
remember the chief features of the teaching of this sect.
In doing so, it is necessary to discriminate between the
teaching of Mani and that of Faustus, one of the Bishops
of this sect, who was a native of North Africa and who
could scarcely be expected to read the sacred books of his
religion in the original Aramaic. Many scholars think that
Faustus taught a base form of the original teaching of the
sect and that the charges brought against the teaching in
Contra Faustum does not represent the true doctrine of
Mani.

Manichaeism was not a heresy in the same way as
Arianism and Pelagianism. It did not originate within the
Church. Mani, the founder, a Persian, was born A.D. 215.
His brief career continued from about A.D. 240 to A.D. 270.
St. Augustine tells us that both supporters and opponents
played upon his name, the former emphasising the
similarity of his name to that of the Heavenly Manna,[1]
the latter finding in the name a suggestion of madness.

In his Epistles and other works Mani assumed a
peculiar character, invented by himself. He wrote various
books, the titles of which have survived. Among these
are: *The Gospel, The Book of the Giants, The Book of
Making Alive,* and *The Book of First Principles*. One
extant writing *The Foundation* has been ascribed to Mani
himself. Some writings by Faustus also exist. From these

[1] *De Haer.*, 46.

47

works and Augustine's writings we can learn details of the teaching of the sect.

Manichaeism was a species of Oriental Dualism which was widely taught throughout the Roman Empire. There were differences in the mode of teaching in the various localities where it was found. Mani borrowed much from religions with which he was familiar. Authorities differ as to the extent of his borrowing from the religion of Babylonia. Some scholars think that Manichaeism contains elements of Buddhism, but Dr. Burkitt does not believe that Mani was influenced in this direction.[1]

A writer thus describes Manichaeism.[2] "In Manichaeism are to be found elements of Babylonian cosmology, bits of Mazdaism, large slices of Gnostic speculation (especially that of Marcion and of Bardesanes), a pinch of Buddhism, crumbs from the Mandaeans, Cainites, and Nicolaitans, and that main prop of Montanism, the descent of the Paraclete or Holy Spirit; but instead of entering into Montanus, the Third Person had become incarnate in the son of Futak Babak. To sum up: this creed was a *contamination* of Zoroaster and Christ—an exaggerated Zoroaster and a misrepresented Christ—and was rendered still more mischievous by trimmings and condiments borrowed from all the heresies."

Their Church consisted of a Prince, as its head, twelve Apostles or Masters, and seventy-two Bishops, called "the sons of the Intelligence," who ordained presbyters and deacons. Next in order came the Manichee believers, who were divided into monks and laymen, or, as the Manichees called them, the "Elect" and the "Hearers" or "Auditors." The former were the true Manichees. The

---

[1] F. C. Burkitt. *Religion of the Manichees*, p. 44.
[2] Giovanni Papini. *Saint Augustine*, p. 58.

latter were no more than adherents. The number of the "Elect" was comparatively small and the renunciations exacted from them were severe. All Manichees were vegetarians, but the Elect abstained from wine, from marriage, and from the ownership of property. They were expected to live a nomadic life, possessing no more than food for a day and clothes for a year.[1] Their obligations not to produce fresh life or to take it was so absolute that it extended even to the vegetable kingdom. "They durst pluck no flower nor break a stalk of grass"; they might neither sow nor reap, nor even break their bread themselves, "lest they pain the Light which was mixed with it." To Marcion, as well as to Mani, all generation of life was abhorrent. The only legitimate marriage to the Marcionite was marriage to Christ.

The "Hearers," naturally, constituted the majority of the Manichaean community. They were permitted to marry and hold property, in fact, to live in the world like other folk. These concessions, doubtless, appealed to the weakness of Augustine's nature and, consequently, he preferred to remain an "Auditor."

Their worship was of a simple character, consisting of prayers and hymns. Their houses of prayer contained no altar, pictures, nor statues. Prayer was ordered to be offered four times a day, the supplications being addressed to the Powers of Light, and to the Master, Mani.

Mani called himself the Apostle of Jesus, and regarded himself as the Paraclete whom Jesus had foretold was to restore the true Church. He claimed for himself divine authority and commission. Sunday was observed as a fast-day by ordinary Manichaeans, Monday by the "Elect." Manichaeism had its sacraments, including

[1] Burkitt. *Religion of the Manichees*, p. 45.

D

those of Baptism, without oil, and the Eucharist, without wine.

Faustus made the bold assertion that Manichaeism was the original and genuine form of Christianity and that the Catholic faith was a debased form of Christianity. The followers of Mani were the true Bride of Christ.

In the *Foundation*, Mani affirms that there are two external principles, Light and Darkness; that by the regrettable mixture of Dark and Light this material Universe came into being; and that the aim and object of those who are children of Light is the gradual destruction of this world by the separation of the Light particles from the Dual substance, with which they have been mixed.[1] God the Father presides over the kingdom of Light and a dreadful prince over the latter. The former kingdom is spiritual, the latter material. These two kingdoms are naturally, as in Zoroastrianism, in a state of mutual antagonism.

Faustus, in his writings, argues that the Creator of the things which are good and of those which are evil cannot be identical. He favours the teaching of Dualism. The Creator of all that is good is God, the Creator of evil he names "Hyle." He declares that God is finite. In their system of eschatology, the Manichees taught that the "Elect" would attain to deliverance from the body; the inferior class would experience a species of transmigration and be degraded into lower forms which were chained permanently to earth.

It is not easy to explain what the Manichees mean when they speak of "God," for to them "God" is a substance rather than a Person, using these expressive terms in their modern connotation. Faustus, however, expounding his

[1] Burkitt. *Religion of the Manichees*, p. 4.

conception of God, uses Trinitarian phrases. "We worship," he writes, "one deity, under the threefold title ("appellatione") of the Almighty God the Father, and His Son Christ, and of the Holy Spirit. While these are one and the same, we believe also that the Father properly dwells in the highest or principal light, which Paul calls light inaccessible, and the Son is His second or visible light. And as the Son is Himself twofold, according to the Apostle, who speaks of Christ as the power of God and the wisdom of God, we believe that His power dwells in the sun, and His wisdom in the moon. We also believe that the Holy Spirit, the third Majesty, has His seat and His home in the whole circle of the atmosphere."[1]

Dr. Burkitt considers that they thought of God as a Quarternity, according to their four-fold conception of God—God, His Light, His Power, His revealed Wisdom.

The "Jesus" revered by Mani has a nature different from the Jesus Christ of orthodox Christianity and also from the Jesus of the Gospels. Jesus in Mani's system seems to occupy a peculiar position among the hierarchy of Light. He was the last of the series of created beings before Mani, but he was more than that. He was a Divine Being, but owing to the Manichaean teaching that matter is identified with evil, Faustus was compelled to deny that Christ was incarnate. To be born of a woman would mean contamination with evil. The Incarnation, as we accept it, was in contradiction to their Dualistic teaching. Faustus was quite frank in his conclusions. "I disbelieve the Incarnation," he writes. He was thus compelled to invent a theory in connection with the Divinity of Christ. He taught that the Son of Mary was

[1] *Cont. Faust.*, xx, 2.

made Son of God at His Baptism. There was an
association between the two natures of Christ, but it
was not of an intimate character. It was little more
than a friendly condescension on the part of the Son
of God to the Son of Mary. It will thus be realized
that the whole Catholic story of the life of Christ
was set at nought. Christ was not born. He could
not become man. He did not actually die. The Christian
believed that Jesus had been really crucified, but that
was their carnal error. He underwent the experience of
humanity only in appearance. In a word, he was a
phantom.

The African sect of the Manichees appears to have
repudiated very strongly the Jewish religion. It rejected
the Old Testament as being the work of the Devil. The
God of the Jewish people was very different from their
God. "In the God of the Hebrews," writes Faustus, "we
have no interest whatever." Again, he says: "We who
have been converted to Christ from heathenism look
upon the God of the Hebrews not merely as dead, but as
having never existed."[1] They failed utterly to understand
the Old Testament and could not approve of the morals
of the patriarchs. According to Mani, Adam was a
creation of the Powers of Darkness to hinder the
work of the purification of the world. Eve was the representative of sensuality; darkness predominated both in
her soul and body. The one redeeming feature of
the early patriarchs appears to be Seth. The idea
of progressive revelation had not entered the Manichaean
mind.

In rejecting the Old Testament, Mani followed
Marcion, who also rejected it on the ground that it was

[1] *Cont. Faust.*, xv.

not inspired Scripture. The God of the Old Testament, the God of the Jews, was not his God. Mani appears to have adopted Marcion's theory of the origin of man and treated it as mythology.

Even with the teaching of the New Testament, Faustus took great liberties. His followers rejected everything that did not agree with their views. They taught that the text of the New Testament had been deplorably corrupted, especially those passages which they experienced difficulties in reconciling with their teaching. Faustus writes: "Since it is uncertain when these words were spoken, we are at liberty to doubt whether they were spoken at all." Many passages, such as the words: "Christ came to fulfil the Law and the Prophets," Faustus doubted whether Jesus ever spoke at all. Portions of the Gospels were accepted, especially the Sermon on the Mount. The Epistles of St. Paul, they taught, were not interpolated, but Paul was the most enlightened of the Apostles.

Other difficulties presented themselves to Faustus and his friends in trying to reconcile their teaching with that of our Lord and His Apostles. Consequently, he partly acknowledged that there was a difference between his teaching and that of the Christian Church, but he maintained that Christ laid the emphasis on conduct rather than on doctrine, and thus it was possible even to reject the Christian doctrine, providing assent was given to Christian morals.

It will thus be recognised that there is a fundamental difference between the teaching of Mani and that of Christianity. That of Mani can best be described as Oriental Dualism in an extreme form, clothed and expressed in terms of the Catholic faith.

(ii) St. Augustine attracted to Manichaeism

When the mind of Augustine was awakening to the claims of religion, the teaching of Mani was widely diffused in North Africa, and its followers in this region were numerous. Manichaeism had obtained a firm footing, especially in Carthage where many young students were pursuing their studies. The Manichees occupied an exalted position in the intellectual life of the time; many of their number were well educated and attended grammar schools and lectures on rhetoric. They professed to represent classical culture; above all, they made themselves conspicuous by their austere living and religious observances. They also carried on a very active propaganda and endeavoured to persuade journalists and others to bring their tenets to the front, with a view to promote public discussion.[1]

This system of teaching would, naturally, be very disturbing to one who was seeking for a reasonable philosophy and a firm faith, and it is easy to understand why Augustine was attracted to the followers of Mani. In the first place, it is obvious that he was not at this time very strongly attached to the Christian faith. His religious outlook must have been disturbed by the mutually opposing belief of his heathen father and his Christian mother. Augustine's education had been pagan to a considerable degree. He was a victim to intellectual pride. The Church at Tagaste was hardly satisfactory to the yearnings of the brilliant mind of this young scholar. He could not therefore resist the attraction of the strange teaching of the Manichaeans. He, doubtless, experienced a difficulty in believing that God was the originator of evil, as his Christian education had not yet taught him

[1] Alfaric. *L'évolution intellectuelle de Saint Augustin*, p. 73.

that evil had not a divine origin. His superficial knowledge of Christian truth had not solved the problem, and the teaching of Dualism, which relieved man of the responsibility for his own sinfulness[1] appears to have overcome some of the difficulties that confronted him. We must emphasise that this religion, in spite of its mythology, was a serious attempt to solve the problem of evil and, as such, it commended itself to Augustine's favour. Manichaeism attempted to explain the existence of evil. Accordingly, in this satisfying system, Augustine found something more attractive than the shallow and unsubstantial moral philosophy current in the schools of rhetoric, namely, a systematic cosmology. It provided a solution—claiming to be "rational"—of the world problem viewed as a whole; in a word, it furnished an explanation of the meaning of life. In fact, Manichaeism professed to give that teaching of which the world stood in need—an authoritative revelation of truth and a coherent doctrine of redemption. It appealed to some thoughtful inquirers as an organised system of practical religion. It made magnificent promises about the acquisition of knowledge.[2] It appeared to offer a religion suited to the needs of the "educated." The words "truth," "science," "reason," were constantly repeated and were believed to be sufficient to attract strangers to become members of their system. Its adherents appeared to experience an inward sympathy with the life of nature. It was a religion superficially Christian in content and in its ethical ideals, yet, at the same time, it was completely "rational" and afforded scope for free inquiry.

[1] *Conf.*, v, 10.
[2] *Conf.*, vi, 5; *De Util. Cred.*, i, 2.

Manichaeism is a Philosophy of the Universe, expressed in terms of Mythology. It made a strong appeal to the imagination of its adherents. It laid the blame on Nature for the evil that men recognise as existing in them, rather than on the human will failing to resist evil promptings.

To the intellectual Augustine, whose awakened curiosity and reason influenced him to find a school that would instruct him in a scientific manner, the Manichaeans promised to explain everything without the intervention of any other authority except that of evidence. He considered it more reasonable to defer to men who offered demonstration than to those who demanded faith. It was this fact that largely decided him to enlist in their ranks. St. Augustine refers to the specious appeal which this system made, in *De Util. Cred.*, i, 2; "You know," he writes, "that we adhered to these men on no other ground than this—that they promised by pure and simple reason to bring their disciples to God, discarding all peremptory authority, and to liberate them from error. For what else made me reject for almost nine years continuously the religion my parents had instilled into me as a child? What else made me a follower and diligent 'hearer' of this sect, than their assertion that we Catholics are terrorised by superstition and that faith is thrust upon us before any reason is given; whereas they constrain none to believe except when the truth is examined and made clear? By such promises, who would not have been inveigled? Especially the mind of a young man, desirous to know the truth, and already, through disputation with clever persons in the schools, grown proud and talkative; just such a one, indeed, as they found *me*—one who condemned religion as an old wives' fable and was eager to apprehend and drink in the very truth which they so confidently promised."

Another thing which probably attracted Augustine to the ranks of the Manichees was the perpetual reiteration of the names of the Holy Trinity and the reverence extended to Christ by them when they termed Him the Son of the Living God, and, also, the subtle use they made of St. Paul's language which would allure an inadequately instructed Christian. Furthermore, the Catholic Church at Carthage was much divided by the Donatist controversy and, consequently, Manichaeism profited by the weakness of the Christian Church in that city.

(iii) Augustine becomes dissatisfied with Manichaeism

Augustine made his spiritual home with the adherents of Manichaeism for nine years, but towards the latter part of this time he began to discover that this religion was not all that it had professed to be; neither was Faustus the intellectual genius that Augustine had expected to find in him. There were many things, he states, which, on later reflection, ought to have prevented this rapid and willing abandonment of the religion of his youth.[1]

It is clear that Augustine had at first only imperfectly understood the teachings of the sect. He soon began to realise that there were phases of its teaching to which he could not give a whole-hearted approval. He could not, for instance, reconcile himself to its mythology, nor to the practice of worshipping the sun. He believed, however, that these points were non-essentials and that it was better for him to give the new religion the benefit of the

[1] De Duab. Anim., i.

doubt, thinking that there were hidden truths in this system of devotion which he had not fathomed and which would be revealed to him as time passed.[1]

Augustine does not appear to have realised that he was inconsistent in his charitable views of the religion of Mani by regarding it with the eyes of faith without demonstration—an attitude which he refused to adopt towards Christianity and towards Christ.

Augustine mentions another feature of Manichaean devotion which affected him painfully.[2] As a boy he had been accustomed to observe the Festival of Easter with great joy as the queen of Christian festivals. Although the "Festival of Bema" was held in great honour by the Manichaeans, yet Easter Day passed almost unnoticed by them. Augustine could not, at the time, appreciate the reason for this neglect but he realised that it was in consequence of the Dualistic principles of Faustus that the life of Christ had been reduced to unreality. According to its teaching, Christ was not really born, therefore He could not actually die, nor could He rise again.

At a public disputation in Carthage, when Helpidus, a Christian advocate, was the chief speaker, some strong Scripture evidence was brought forward for the Christian faith which the Manichees were not able to answer, except by denying that the Scripture passages were genuine. The followers of Mani asserted that the Christian Scriptures had been corrupted by the Jews, but, on being challenged for evidence, were unable to substantiate their statements. Many of the more intelligent "hearers" clearly recognised that the Manichees were unable to

[1] *De Beat. Vit.*, iv.
[2] *C. Ep. Fund.*, viii 9.

maintain their principles, and this fact set Augustine thinking. His reflection led him to doubt whether evil was a substance after all. Time only increased his difficulties, and even the arrival in Carthage of Faustus, the champion of the Manichaean religion, did not convince him of the trustworthiness of many of the particulars of their theology. The motive of evil as a substance co-eternal with God could not satisfy his spirit in its struggle after unity. Faustus, also, had argued that morals took precedence of theological ideas. Augustine thought differently and the encounter only served to loosen still more the ties which held Augustine to the Manichaean faith.

Oriental Dualism was not destined to be Augustine's resting-place. His study of Aristotle was, probably, a most potent factor influencing his change of mind. As Professor Harnack points out, his innate tendency towards "the empirical and the real won the victory, so soon as Aristotle—the great logician and inquirer into Nature—came to his aid."[1] He discovered that the vaunted explanations of the Manichaeans were mythological and conflicted with what he knew of astronomy, and it was this fact which considerably weakened the hold of Manichaeism upon him.

Augustine's ideal of chastity and self-restraint which he then recognised as promising a foretaste of union with God, failed to deliver him from the fetters of sensuality. Although he was not able to realise his lofty ideal, everything which Manichaeism seemed to offer him faded away as the result of his criticism. The more he learned the more fully he recognised the incompatibility of Manichaean astrology with facts.

[1] Harnack. *Augustin's Konfessionem*, p. 20.

When he attempted to solve the problems of psychology, he became convinced of the insufficiency of Manichaean astrology. As he studied the problems of psychology more deeply, he recognised the unsatisfactory nature of Dualism, which now appeared to him incapable of solving the most important questions.

He, finally, came to the conclusion that the Manichaean propaganda was invertebrate and wanting in force. His discussion with Faustus resulted in his complete disillusionment. His mental conflict convinced him of the evil of human nature, and Manichaeism had left him in complete doubt as to the foundations and truth of the Christian faith. His confidence in the rationality of Christian truth had been shaken to the very depths, and it was never restored. In other words, as an individual thinker he never gained the subjective certitude that Christian truth and, consequently, everything contained in the two Testaments, must be regarded as clear, consistent and demonstrable. This mutual conflict changed his whole outlook. In the teaching of St. Augustine, accordingly, experience led to remarkable conclusions. His decision to find a home in Rome brought this chapter of his history to a close, and for a time he took refuge in scepticism.

(iv) Influence of Manichaeism as it appears in Augustine's writings

Professor Harnack's assertion that Augustine never wholly lost sight of Manichaeism is certainly true.[1] We find traces of it in these familiar antitheses which we read in the teaching of St. Paul and to which Augustine gave

[1] See Harnack. Hist. of Dogma, v, p. 102, and note on p. 211; also Fairbairn, Christ in Modern Theology, pp. 115, fol.

currency in Western theology: nature and grace, divine predestination and human freedom. It is also seen in the contrasted conceptions of Augustine's *Civitas Dei*, ultimately identified with the Church and the *Civitas Mundi*, which appeared to be represented by Imperial Rome. It is in these contrasts that we discern a perceptible reflexion of the Manichaean notion of the eternal realms of Light and Darkness.

There is also, we venture to think, a remnant of Manichaean thought in Augustine's moral theology: in his outlook on marriage, his undue exaltation of virginity, and in his severely ascetic conception of holiness. Celibacy, to Augustine, is an infinitely higher state than wedded life. Even the possession of property is regarded not as a means of fulfilling social duty, but as a hindrance to the spiritual life of the individual.

Augustine mentions that the Manichaeans are obsessed by the idea of evil: "While they devote themselves over-much to the problem 'Whence is evil?' they discover nothing but evil."[1] Yet it is obvious to the reader of Augustine's works that there is a decided tendency to pessimism in his idea of the world. He emphasises the importance of detachment from the world and its concerns as a supreme duty. He sees evil supreme in physical nature and pre-eminently in the sphere of sexual relationships. He appears to forget that the world, being the handiwork of God, is good. Eucken observes that, so far as his influence extends, an element of Manichaeism was grafted upon Christianity, and this is apt to assert itself to this day.[2] Augustine's celebrated passage: "For who is sufficient, with whatsoever torrent of eloquence he

[1] *De Util. Cred.*, xviii, 3.
[2] Eucken. *The Problem of Human Life*, p. 229.

? historical circumstances !

possesses, to set forth at length the miseries of this present life?"[1] helps us to see how over-strained is Augustine's sense of the dominance of evil in human life.

It has been pointed out that Augustine wrote his *De Civitate* in days when the whole fabric of civilisation appeared to be tottering to its fall.[2] Nevertheless, he seems to think that there is an impassable gulf fixed between the two societies—the "Civitas Dei" and the earthly commonwealth. He regards the Empire as the very embodiment of evil—as a great brigandage" ("grande latrocinium"), as "the mystic Babylon," and as a very "Kingdom of the devil." Whatever is good in the State, and whatever makes for its stability, he claims for the true "civitas," the Church.[3]

The influence of Manichaeism on Augustine is seen especially in his ideas of the origin of evil. He does not know how the evil Will came into existence.[4] In Chapter xi of his *De Civitate Dei*, he shows that the angels must have been created before the stars and quotes Job xxxviii, 7: "When the morning stars sang together, and all the sons of God shouted for joy." They were created when God said: "Let there be Light"[5]; and when He divided the Light and the Darkness He distinguished between the good and the bad Angels[6] for Satan fell at once, though the evil was not immediately apparent.[7]

---

[1] *De. Civ. Dei*, xix, 4–8.

[2] R. L. Ottley. *Studies in the Confessions of St. Augustine*, p. 53.

[3] Robertson. *Regnum Dei*, pp. 209, *seq.*

[4] *De Civ. Dei*, xii, 7.

[5] *De Civ. Dei*, xi, 9.

[6] xi, 19, 33.

[7] *Cf. De Civ. Dei*, xi, 19.

"God made two great lights, the greater light to rule the day, and the lesser light to rule the night . . . and God set them in the firmament of heaven . . . but between that light which is the holy society of angels, shining in the lustre of intelligible truth and their opposite darkness, the wicked angels, perversely fallen from that light of justice, He could only make separation. *Cf.* also *De Civ. Dei*, xi, 33. "These two societies, the one enjoying God, the other swelling in pride . . . the one inflamed with God's love, the other, blown big with self-love."

Thus, according to this view, evil came about by pride before man was created. According to Augustine, man was formed in a universe where there were already two powers, God and Satan, and in the first conflict between these two principles of Light and Darkness the first man came to grief.

This corresponds to the Manichaean teaching on the subject. There are other traces of the doctrine of Mani in the eleventh book of this great work. Augustine knew that Darkness was no more than the absence of Light, but, for all that, when in xi, 33 he is making a contrast between the two Angelical societies, the one "tranquil in its luminous piety," the other "turbulent with its dark cupidities and smoking with the unclean mouth of its own loftiness," he uses language with a curiously Manichaean ring. And while he was teaching in this fashion he was influencing the imaginations of fifty generations to come. The learned interpretation of Augustine passed into the poetical conceptions of Aritus, the teaching of Columba, and finally (with characteristic perversion) into the writings of Milton.[1]

1 Burkitt. *Religion of the Manichees*, p. 103.

(v) Augustine opposes Manichaeism

A remarkable change in his views took place while Augustine was in Rome. He began to form a clear estimate of the relative value of Christianity and Manichaeism. He wrote two books on the morals of the Catholic Church and of the Manichaeans.[1] He was engaged in this controversy for many years and wrote many treatises including *De Genesi contra Manichaeos*, *De actis cum Felice Manichaeo*, and *Contra Fortunatum*. The most outstanding of these writings is the elaborate reply to his old associate and disputant, Faustus of Mileve.[2]

The Manichaean heresy had for a long time enslaved the mind of Augustine; consequently, it was only natural that his great mental powers as a theological thinker and controversialist should concentrate on this erroneous system. He supplemented his arguments on the unity of Creation and of the spiritual life with proofs from his own experience. He inspired and encouraged the Christian Church in her last struggle with that dualistic spirit, which animated and moulded, in succession, so many forms of thought at variance with the truths of the religion of Jesus Christ.

[1] *De moribus ecclesiae Catholicae et de moribus Manichaeorum libri duo.*

[2] *Contra Faustum Manichaeum.* A.D. 400.

CHAPTER IV

ST. AUGUSTINE'S WRITINGS

ST. AUGUSTINE is the most prolific author of all the Latin Church Fathers. Possidius asserts that his writings, including sermons and letters, reached the total of 1,030. He gives his views in every department of theology. He wrote, not with the intention of acquiring literary fame, but influenced by the promptings of his heart, and moved by his love towards God and Man. His learning is not equal to that of Origen or Jerome; but in originality, depth, and expressiveness of soul, he is greater than all the Greek and Latin Fathers. His forcefulness does not depend on his knowledge of Hebrew and Greek, for he read Greek with difficulty, and, as for Hebrew, he knew but little; all we learn on this subject from the recent studies of Schanz and Rothmanner is that he was familiar with Punic, a language resembling Hebrew in some respects. His historical and grammatical exegeses were not satisfactory, for the simple reason that his intense feeling and remarkable subtlety often compelled him to give interpretations that were strained or more ingenious than satisfactory. We recognise that he is at his best in the development of theological and religious thought, more especially in his minute and accurate psychological observation.

In this chapter we desire to indicate and summarise the chief sources of information he made use of in his psychological studies. His teaching on psychological subjects can be found not only in his philosophical treatises, but also in his Letters, and his polemic and dogmatic writings.

It is not necessary to refer to every treatise of this great writer which deals with questions concerning the human soul; we can only refer to the most important of his writings which have a more direct bearing on our subject.

The literary career of this great Father continued for more than forty-four years and in that time his views underwent considerable change; it is important, therefore, to remember that if we wish to interpret his doctrine on every subject in an intelligent and accurate manner, we must be careful to attend to the historical order and literary setting of his writings. He tells us that his writings were of a progressive nature as his knowledge increased as he wrote; in the Prologue of the *Retractationes* he says that, in order to understand the development of his doctrine, his treatises should be studied in the order in which they were written. The influence of the Neo-Platonic method of thought is evident in many of the treatises written at Rome and at Tagaste. Neo-Platonism was for him, as for many others, the star which guided him into the fold of Christianity. For an intelligent understanding of his works it is, accordingly, important to bear in mind their chronological order and the phase of his spiritual development at the time of writing.

De Ordine

The two books which are called *De Ordine* were composed at Cassiciacum at the close of A.D. 386. They are dedicated to Zenobius, one of his intimate companions. Divine Providence and the Order of the Universe are the chief topics discussed in this treatise. In Book II he treats of such questions as the relation of philosophy to theology;[1] authority and reason;[2] "quid sit Ratio?";[3] quo

[1] Ch. v.   [2] Ch. ix.   [3] Ch. xi.

ordine anima provehitur ad cognitionem sui et ipsius unitatis;[1] homo unde brutis praestantior?"[2].

Soliloquies

The date of the *Soliloquies* is earlier than that of the *Confessions*. They were written during the time which elapsed between his conversion and his baptism; this was while he was in a state of spiritual transition. This book, consequently, contains an accurate record of his theological progress at that time. The *Soliloquies* are written in the form of a dialogue, in which Augustine represents himself as discussing certain questions with his own reason. They open with a fervent prayer; then his pent up feelings of devotion are released. He discusses the qualities of mind and heart requisite for seeing a vision of God. The name of God is mentioned over and over again, and each time with the suggestion of some new idea about the Divine nature.

In the *Soliloquies* the supremacy of reason is called in question as the result of his passionate desire to know God. "I know not," he writes, "how any rational demonstration of God could satisfy; for I believe that I do not know anything as I desire to know God." Augustine has advanced beyond the philosophical conception of God to believe in the God of the Christians. He now enjoys fellowship with a personal Being, and no longer with an abstract Deity. He lifts up his heart, and prays: "Hear me, hear me, hear me, my God, my Lord, my King, my Father, my Creator, my hope, my possession, my glory, my home, my country, my salvation, my light, my life."

Augustine was in a very emotional condition of mind when he wrote his *Soliloquies*, as he felt deeply humiliated

[1] Ch. xviii.   [2] Ch. xix.

by his consciousness of past inconsistencies. Influenced by his emotions, he undertakes a severe self-examination concerning his purpose in life, and seriously analyses his motives as regards his ambition, the desire to be rich, and his views on the subject of marriage. During this process of severe self-analysis, he turns, from time to time, to prayer, and refers to it in the words, "God, Who art always the same, let me know myself, let me know Thee."

One of the subjects discussed is that of truth—its unchangeable character and its relation to consciousness; this leads him on to think of the immortality of man. The imperishable nature of truth implies the immortality of its exponent. God and the soul remain, because the soul is the dwelling-place of immortal truth. Truth cannot die. Therefore we must not doubt the everlasting existence of the mind. Knowledge is in the mind, and physical death cannot cause the mind to perish. If it could, then truth also could perish, which is impossible.

To Augustine, truth had no existence apart from the mind. He appears, however, to realise the weakness of his inference that the permanence of truth requires the permanence of the human mind which contemplates it. Again, he does not really face the question: "where was the home of truth before the existence of man?" He does not even hint that the home of everlasting truth may have been in the eternal mind of God.

Augustine appears to arrive at the conclusion that reason by itself is not adequate to bring the soul to God. The entire personality is necessary, and this includes the will as well as the intellect. Thus, the writer dissents from the previous thesis he maintained, when he exclaims: "I have nothing else than my will."

De Quantitate Animae

The treatise *De Quantitate Animae* is in the form of a dialogue with a friend named Euodius, and gives an account of discussions on the following questions in reference to the human soul: "Unde sit?" "qualis sit?" "quanta sit?" "cur corpori fuerit data?" "cum ad corpus venerit qualis efficiatur?" "qualis cum abscesserit?" The greater portion of the work is devoted to an examination of the question: "Quanta sit anima?" According to Augustine, the human soul is a simple substance; that is to say, it is unextended; it does not occupy space like material objects, so that different aspects of the soul correspond to different parts of space; but it is present in the body which it animates "vi ac potentia"[1] The last four chapters deal with the seven stages in the progress of the individual soul towards God—an idea borrowed from Neo-Platonism.

De Libero Arbitrio. Lib. III

The second and third books of *De Libero Arbitrio* were written about A.D. 395 in Hippo. The first book of this work was written about the year A.D. 388, while Augustine was sojourning at Rome. They contain a series of dialogues with his friend Euodius, in which they discuss the problem of evil and its relation to the liberty of the individual. This treatise was intended primarily as a refutation of the Manichaean tenet that God is the author of evil as well as of good. He maintains against the Manichaeans, that God is not the author of evil, but that evil exists in consequence of man's exercise of free will. Chapters xx and xxi of Book III give a concise statement of Augustine's difficulties regarding the origin of the

[1] Ch. xxxii, 69.

souls of the descendants of the first man. Up to this time Augustine has always hesitated about taking a definite stand in reference to this question, but he seems to have inclined to favour the theory of Traducianism as it appeared to be the one most reconcilable with the orthodox doctrine of original sin.

Augustine also desires to justify his hesitancy in expressing himself definitely upon the manner of the soul's origin in *De Anima et ejus Origine*.

De Musica

Augustine read widely on the subject of the arts and began to write treatises on them. Only four books of the treatise, *De Musica*, have survived. They contain a remarkable analysis of the various possibilities in poetical expression; the subjects he treats of are rhythm, metre, and verse. Although the illustrations in the earlier part of the treatise are taken from classical poetry—Terence, Horace, and Vergil—in the last book there is a hymn of Ambrose.

Although the subject matter is simple, yet in his treatment there is a considerable amount of profound philosophy and psychology; there is also the first suggestive outline of the theory of aesthetics which influenced the culture of Europe for centuries.

To Augustine, the teaching of music meant nothing else than using the harmonies of sensation, in order to lead the spirit to the discovery of the Invisible.

In this treatise, for the first time in the writings of Augustine, is found the doctrine of the Fall of Man. The idea of human nature degenerating through the action of sin and the subjection of man to corruption and death are now part of Augustine's system of teaching. Here also appears the doctrinal cure for human frailty in the divinely chosen method of Redemption. There are certain evidences that the doctrine of the Incarnation was assuming greater importance in Augustine's mind, as he taught the dogma that the divine Wisdom, by an amazing and ineffable act of condescension, assumed the sinner's nature without being contaminated by his sin.

We also discover the thought that, if the soul forsakes the Master, who is God, to become the servant of the body, with its passions and desires, it necessarily deteriorates. When it turns from the service of the body to the Master, by the same necessity it improves. The former is an inversion of its natural order and destiny. The soul should rule its inferior, and be ruled by its superior, that is, God.[1]

De Vera Religione

This treatise was written about A.D. 390, while Augustine was a layman, and only three years after his baptism. The newly-made convert was anxious to convince Romanian, his friend, who had followed his example in accepting the theory of Dualism, about the true religion.

Although there is no clear systematic treatment of the subject, yet Augustine has bequeathed a profusion of ideas and considerable stores of thought. He is bold enough to state that, if Plato returned to this world he would find that the Christian religion would satisfy his aspirations. It would need only the change of a few words of Christian teaching to attract Plato into the Church of Christ.

This treatise is not only an argument against idolatry

[1] W. S. Simpson. *St. Augustine's Conversion*, p. 199.

and heresy, but also a synopsis of Augustine's belief, an epitome that comes, with great enthusiasm, from the depths of his heart. It is a document that attests his complete allegiance to Christianity. He is now no longer a pupil, but a teacher of the Church, and he stands up in her defence.

Augustine treats of the Christian doctrine of the origin of evil, and refutes the theory which ascribed the origin of evil to the existence of a substance inherently evil; all life and everything that exists proceed from God, for God is the supreme existence, and the Author of all existence. No life, he points out, as far as it is life, is evil; but only as far as it tends to death. Evil is the very opposite and negation of existence. Evil is a perverse action of the will. It is the result of moral choice. There is no such thing as an evil nature. Evil is the result of man's own fault.

Augustine also explains, for the benefit of his friend, the process by which he had been converted. The two methods for the acquisition of truth, he points out, are authority and reason. Authority demands faith as man's response to the call of God, and also prepares the way for reason; in dealing with the latter he sets forth his problem of the Beautiful. He adds that to many the only important thing is the delight which the beautiful conveys to them, rather than the inquiry as to why it is that things beautiful delight them. The true use of created things is made when the mind ascends through the creature to the Uncreated.

Augustine shows that beauty, goodness, and unity are not borrowed from sensible things. On the contrary, sensible things have received these perfections from above, and it is because we know them dimly within ourselves that we are able to know and measure the sensible beauty and order of things. Then from these interior experiences we are able to recognise the absolute beauty and unity, which is God.

In his search for truth Augustine exclaims: "Look not beyond yourself. Return within, truth dwells in the inner man, and," he adds, "if you find your own nature to be changeable, transcend also yourself."

There is a wealth of Christian terminology in the latter portion of this treatise. We read of omnipotence, and the Trinity of one substance, and the grace whereby we are reconciled, and even if the freedom of the will is stated in terms somewhat unguarded, these are afterwards corrected and qualified. "The wealth of thought, the depth of insight, the beautiful exposition of the significance of the beautiful, all give evidence of the fascinating power of the religious genius of Augustine."[1]

De Utilitate Credendi

This treatise was written by Augustine for the enlightenment of another of his friends, Honoratus, whom, also, he had led into Dualism, and whom he now wished to bring into the Christian Church by persuading him of the immense superiority of the Catholic religion. The book is virtually a personal record of the development of Augustine's belief and experience, and, consequently, it enriches our knowledge about his advance in religious conviction.

After expressing his great desire to discover the truth, he explains how he was enticed by specious pretensions of the followers of Mani to bring men to the knowledge of God; their intellectual discussions, without any reference to the claims of faith, resulted in his becoming an

[1] W. S. Simpson. *St. Augustine's Conversion*, p. 221.

adherent of their Dualistic religion. Although he lived in an arrogant and unsettled age, yet there were certain compensations in the fact that he lived in a University atmosphere. In time, however, he began to discover that this religion was more destructive than constructive, and gradually he came to realise by experience the limitations of human reason. He explains how he came to understand that the principles of true religion must first be accepted by faith, and afterwards tested by experience. Authority, and its correlative faith, must precede the personal apprehension of religious truth. Augustine points out that it is impossible to eliminate the need of faith from ordinary life, such as in friendship. What can be more reasonable, he asks, than to accept by faith those things which are divinely constituted to prepare the mind for truth. To refuse the assent of faith is surely to be a danger to oneself and a warning to others. Unless we exercise faith, and so absorb into our minds the germs of truth, which our reason is unable to explain, there is little prospect of restoring our weakened capacities to health and vigour.

Faith is thus the means by which wisdom is received; although by exercising faith we risk being deceived, yet it is the greater folly to exercise no faith.

Although faith may be said to be the more important factor in our religious life, yet he assigns to Reason a position of superiority. The two terms are not antagonistic as faith and reason go hand in hand. We must aspire to certify by reason what we accept by faith. Faith will ever be a life-long necessity.

The Confessions

Although it is fifteen centuries since Augustine wrote, yet the *Confessions* are still regarded by Christian people as a religious classic, as a remarkable contribution to theology, and, it may be added, to psychology.

In medieval times the *City of God* was, doubtless, more popular, but to-day the *Confessions* are regarded as the more important contribution to thought. To-day, psycho-analysis interests us more than the philosophy of history; we are less metaphysical and more psychological than our forefathers.

The *Confessions* is a treatise which is remarkable for its originality. It is neither a formal treatise on psychology nor an abstract inquiry into the nature of the soul; it does not resemble the *Meditations* of Marcus Aurelius, which is the result of mere moralising self-analysis; it is not like the *Faust* of Goethe, the utterance of ineffectual yearnings or the pursuit of unattainable ideals. Augustine's treatise simply described the aspirations of a human soul, its moods of abasement and exaltation, the bitterness of its conflicts, and the ardour of a spiritual quest for peace and joy. It is unique in its appeals, its self-disclosure and its account of a man's discovery of God. The book, certainly, owes its charm to its transparent sincerity. Like the penitents in primitive times who publicly confessed their guilt in the presence of the assembled Church, so Augustine lays bare to the reader the very secrets of his heart. Although he looks back at the past through the medium of the opinions and impressions of his later days, yet his one great aim is to give a wholly faithful and honest description of his soul's history. It is not surprising, therefore, that his writings have appealed so strongly to the religious instincts of man in every age, so strongly, indeed, that no one can estimate the importance of their influence.

In the *Confessions*, the reader can find speculation and

introspective theology and autobiography, and his account of God and the "ego." After the study of this remarkable volume, we arrive at the conclusion that Augustine was the last of the great metaphysicians of antiquity and the first of modern psychologists.

Augustine had no desire for ostentation when writing this treatise. He informs us in his *Retractations* what was his motive: "The thirteen books of my *Confessions* praise a just and merciful God for all my blessings and for all that in any way affects me; they lift up the heart of man to Him." No work of his has been more universally read and admired; none, certainly, has caused more tears to flow than this searching book. It is a remarkable analysis of the most complex workings of the soul. As an expression of deep feeling, elevation of sentiment, and comprehension of philosophic outlook, there is no book like it in all literature. In it is revealed a soul which is gradually healed by the mercy of the Divine Physician.

The subject matter of the *Confessions* is, indeed, difficult, as it is, for the most part, an account of a man's inner experience. Two peculiarities explain the extraordinary interest it awakes—his unusual powers of introspection and his interest in what is taking place in the external world. His power of introspection enables him to describe the working of his inner self in such a vivid manner. His keen sense of sight and hearing enables him to describe the outward world in a striking manner to others. His descriptions are vivid chiefly because of his use of metaphors.

In his polemical tractates, his dialogues, his letters, and his sermons, Augustine always addresses some unseen listeners; the *Confessions* is a lengthy epistle addressed to God. He mentions persons by name only when they enable him to explain something which concerns himself. The *Confessions* may be described as the true reflection of the mind of the writer. His examination of conscience recognises the presence of the Absolute. It is, certainly, his great literary masterpiece.

The first ten books are an intimate description of the author's mental and moral experiences from his infancy to the time of his conversion. He describes his first half-hearted efforts to turn from the things of sense as follows: "The pressure of the world lay heavy upon me like a feeling of drowsiness which is not altogether unpleasant, and my thoughts, when I strove to raise them to Thee, were like the efforts of a man trying to awaken, but constantly falling back into slumber."

The last three books are exegetical in character, being chiefly a commentary on the history of the Creation as recorded in the Book of Genesis. The autobiographical part of the work especially reveals the remarkable introspective powers of the author, and his ability to describe the workings of his mind. The tenth book is a subtle analysis of Memory and Remembering—a fine contribution to psychology. This treatise is most useful because he bases an argument for the spirituality of the soul on the power of Memory. The work as a whole, however, rather than any specific part, contains many useful items of information, and suggestions which help the reader to understand Augustine's concept of the human soul.

The *Retractations* assert that Augustine's purpose in writing the *Confessions* was to address a hymn of praise to God through the confession of man. We must, however, ask whether this was the only motive which influenced Augustine to write them. The question also arises—why did he wish to praise God in this way at this particular time?

Some think that he wrote the *Confessions* at the instance of his friends; on examination, however, we learn that his earnest desire for grace is emphasised, and this, and the longing for the prayers of his readers, induced him to write this treatise. On further investigation of the contents, however, we discover two complexes at work in his longing for grace. It is the complex of sin on the one hand, and of grace on the other. These complexes apparently influenced the spiritual outlook of Augustine, and this is a sufficient explanation of his motives in writing this treatise.

De Trinitate

This is one of the most profound of Augustine's dogmatic treatises. The time of writing extended over a period of fifteen years. In it we have a record of Augustine's reflections on the Incarnation and on the Holy Trinity. It was written when he was a faithful member of the Christian Church and, consequently, it contains his well-matured conclusions on some important dogmas.

His motive in writing this treatise was to teach that those who desired to demonstrate the truth of these dogmas by reason alone are in error; he asserts that the human mind is incapable of understanding the nature of God, and, therefore, the doctrine of the Trinity can be comprehended by faith and not by reason.

He was influenced to treat of this subject, not because he especially wished to do so, but because his clergy complained that most of the literature on the subject was in Greek, which they could not read. In the second place, he was not attracted by the subject because his method of treatment was that of a thinker whose mind moves most easily in the concrete. The *De Trinitate* is frequently referred to, and quoted from, on account of its analogies.

He tells us that the Incarnation implies the self-humiliation of God. He does not fully explain his teaching on this subject in one part of his exposition, but it occurs here and there throughout the treatise. He appears at times to quote from the Athanasian Creed, perhaps in its early form.

We frequently observe in the writings of Augustine that the expression of his ideas is too rapid to allow him to express his theories in a systematic manner. This characteristic is especially noticeable in the treatise *De Trinitate*, where the author, after mentioning an idea, abandons it as if the current of his thoughts was interrupted, but returns to the subject again later on.

One special feature of this treatise is the number of psychological illustrations given, such as memory, understanding, and will, which are described as the trinities of thought;[1] Augustine considers them to be inadequate representations of the subject. His references to nature— for example, the gliding of a snake[2]—help us to understand his outlook.

Equally noteworthy are his remarks on the consciousness of an infant, and its interest in seeing a light,[3] and, again, on the nature of vision.[4] In Chapters ix–xv he skilfully examines the various trinities which are found in man.

The ontological proof of the existence of God has often been ascribed to Anselm, but a study of *De Trinitate*, viii, proves that Anselm was indebted to Augustine for the basic principles of his argument.

[1] xi, 11. [2] xii, 16. [3] xiv, 7. [4] xi, 4.

The freedom of the will is also discussed in this treatise. Fallen man, Augustine asserts, has not lost the power of will, but it is a base and "servile freedom" of yielding willingly to the instincts of his lower nature. "Nam et animae in ipsis peccatis suis non nisi quamdam simili-tudinem Dei, superba et praepostera, et, ut ita dicem, servile libertate sectantur."[1]

This treatise was one of the sources of the metaphysics of the Middle Ages, and it promoted the technico-logical training of the understanding. The realistic scholasticism of the Middle Ages should not be studied apart from this treatise for the simple reason that it enunciates the principles of Scholasticism.

De Genesi ad Litteram

The composition of this treatise was carried on for more than fourteen years. Its twelve books are chiefly exegetical in character; it upholds the literal interpretation of the first three chapters of the Book of Genesis. The main purpose of the writer is to prove that there is nothing of a historical character recorded in these chapters which cannot be literally true, nothing which is contrary to reason or to the nature of things. Two of these books contain a distinct reference to the problem of the soul; the seventh discusses the nature of the human soul, and the tenth treats of its origin.

In Chapter xi, 14, Augustine refers to the problem of the freedom of the will. He points out that choice depends on motives, and results from a judgment on man's motives: "The reasoning soul yields or refuses assent to interior images by choice of will." Choice, however, according to the teaching of Augustine, is not identical

[1] xi, 8.

with full liberty, as he points out in another of his writings.[1] We may prefer to do what does not, as a matter of fact, lie within our power, whereas liberty implies the power to do what is good.

In Chapter xii, Augustine treats of the theory of the relation of the soul to the body. He says that the soul exists within its own spirituality, but lives united to a body of its own. When something happens to the body, it decides the answer which must be given. Sensation belongs, not to the body, but to the soul through the avenue of the body. He remarks, also, that sensation is a necessary condition to acquire knowledge, but it is equally true that knowledge is not the product of sensation.

The Spirit and the Letter

The title of Augustine's treatise, *The Spirit and the Letter*, is derived from St. Paul's words in II Cor. iii, 6, "not of the letter, but of the spirit: for the letter killeth, but the Spirit giveth life." In a previous treatise, Augustine had used the words in a Pauline sense, but in the treatise, *The Spirit and the Letter*, written some nineteen years later, we find that the letter represents moral instruction and the Spirit is the Holy Spirit at work within the soul. It is an exposition of the Christian doctrine of Grace, and the importance of Grace in reference to the different aspects of Christian truth and Christian experience. It is, certainly, one of Augustine's best compositions. It was written when his mental development was mature, and before he became involved in the Predestinarian controversy. It was written at the request of his friend, Marcellinus.

[1] *De Civ. Dei*, xxii, 30.

F

Augustine believed that the Pelagian theory of Grace was mere intellectualism, and that it failed to appreciate man's moral weakness. The distinction between knowledge and action was strongly overlooked in the Pelagian psychology. Pelagius analysed man's spiritual nature as consisting of capacity, will, and realisation. Capacity or natural endowment was the only part ascribed to God. Augustine taught that God co-operates with man's will and with man's achievements. Dr. Bright[1] says of this treatise that it is a book which, perhaps, next to the *Confessions*, tells us most of the thoughts of that profound and affectionate mind on the soul's relation to its God.

The wonderful psychological power and moral experience of Augustine qualified him to be the chief exponent of the doctrine of Grace, and, therefore, the teaching of this treatise is eminently applicable to human life. Dr. Sparrow Simpson says of it: "The value of the treatise would be difficult to exaggerate. It is profoundly true to the facts of human nature, and to the Christian principles of spiritual development."

De Civitate Dei

The *De Civitate Dei* is an important encyclopaedia of Catholic teaching. It is, unquestionably, the most elaborate, and, in some respects, the most remarkable of his writings. Augustine wrote this treatise because complaints had been alleged against Christianity by the heathen after the invasion and sack of Rome by the Goths in A.D. 410. It is the earliest known effort to formulate a philosophy of history. The writer attempts to vindicate God's character by referring to the events of history. It was, accordingly, written with a definitely controversial aim,

[1] *Introduction to Anti-Pelagian Treatises*, xxi.

to meet a particular need, and at the request of the tribune Marcellinus.

Augustine develops his subject into a comprehensive synthesis, which embraces the history of the whole human race and its destinies in time and eternity. From the first page to the last, he interprets history with persuasive power and insight. It is one of the great writings of Christian antiquity which professedly treats of the relation of the state and of human society in general, in the light of Christian principles. It has exercised, consequently, a wonderful influence on the development of European Christian belief, and especially of political thought. "His apology for Christianity rises at once to the dignity of a magnificent philosophy of history, a work that towers like an Alpine peak over all the other apologies of Christian antiquity."[1]

Augustine, in this treatise, gives the reader a synthesis of universal history in the light of Christian principles. His theory of history is strictly deduced from his dualistic view of human nature, which, in turn, follows necessarily from his teaching on the subject of creation and grace. Its value largely consists of its teaching about the ideal character of the hero, the ideal wisdom of the sage, and the ideal order of the good commonwealth.

Treating of the problem of Divine Providence in reference to the Roman Empire, Augustine extends the apparent boundaries of the horizon and, aided by his genius, writes the philosophy of history. He contemplates the destinies of the world circling around its true centre, the Christian religion, which he regards as the only one which leads humanity on to its most glorious climax.

[1] Bardenhewer-Shahan. *Patrology*, pp. 479–480.

The sociological teaching of Augustine in this treatise is based on the same psychological principles which pervade his thought at all times—the principles of the all-importance of the will and the sovereignty of love.

The two tendencies of the will produce two species of men and two types of society, and so we finally come to the great generalisation of Tyconius, the Donatist, on which Augustine's treatise is founded. "Two loves made the two cities—the earthly, which is built up by the love of self, even to the contempt of God, and the heavenly, which is built up by the love of God which leads even to the contempt of self."[1]

The Augustinian City of God has a certain degree of resemblance to the Neo-Platonic concept of the Intelligible World, yet his Platonism did not influence Augustine to depreciate his sense of the reality and the importance of historical development. It appears that to Origen temporal development had no finality. There was an infinite succession of worlds, through which the immortal soul pursued its endless course. This doctrine Augustine rejected. Time, to him, is not a perpetually changing reflection of eternity; it is an irreversible development moving in a definite direction. This recognition of the uniqueness and irreversibility of the temporal process is one of the most remarkable achievements of Augustine's thought; he may truly be described as "the first man in the world to discover the meaning of time."[2]

In this treatise considerable light is thrown upon the philosophical opinions of the eminent thinkers of

[1] xiv, 28.
[2] C. Dawson. *A monument to St. Augustine*, p. 69.

antiquity. Augustine's doctrine of the human soul is diffused through the whole dissertation. By this treatise and his *Confessions* he is best known. The *City of God* is the highest expression of his thought; the *Confessions* is the best monument of his living piety and Christian experience.

The Retractations

The *Retractations* of Augustine may truly be described as unique; although the revising of a much-read work is nothing new, yet it is very unusual for an author to revise all his treatises.

Augustine, about the year A.D. 412, mentions[1] that he intended to collect into a special book those passages in all his works which displeased him. This step, however, was not taken until fourteen years later. Harnack[2] mentions several facts that would naturally influence Augustine to make this revision; to understand the cause of his action we must assume that there was some motive-complex which impelled him to do so.

This may be explained by his attitude to the doctrines of freedom and grace, on which he laid great emphasis at that time. The Pelagians then tried to play off the old Augustinian doctrines against the new. They believed that they had succeeded in finding certain passages in his former treatises which were inconsistent with his later teaching. For this reason the doctrines of grace and freedom, are discussed. Augustine's arguments seem to be rather unconvincing as he relies upon his rhetorical powers to overcome the opposition of his opponents.

[1] *Ep.*, 143, 2.

[2] *Hist. of Dogma* III, p. 116.

Harnack believes that his polemic would now be considered insincere.

The writing of the *Retractations*, doubtless, somewhat relieved the mind of Augustine and brought peace to his soul.

The *Retractations* contain not only a corrected formulation of his doctrines, but also a justification of his teaching on the subject of grace.

We may see in this action of Augustine the recognition of his great need of vindication and a scrupulous process of self-correction.[1]

In some respects, the *Retractations* may be regarded as a sequel to the *Confessions*. The latter is the story of his life, the former gives an account of his work as Catholic layman, priest, and bishop. In other respects, however, they are very different as they are the result of different motives.

It is, indeed, certain that in his writings Augustine preserves and comments on many of the literary treasures of the old world and transmits them as a precious heritage to posterity. Harnack goes so far as to say: "It would seem that the miserable existence of the Roman Empire in the West was prolonged until then, only to permit Augustine's influence to be exercised on universal history." He, certainly, fulfilled a remarkable task, when Providence brought him into contact with the three worlds, whose thought he was to transmit—with the Roman and Latin world in the midst of which he lived, with the Oriental world partially revealed to him through the study of Manichaeism, and with the Greek world shown to him by the Platonists.

The teaching of Victorinus, Ambrose, Cyprian, and

[1] Legewie. *Augustinus, eine psychographie*, p. 91.

Tertullian, as well as that of pre-Christian writers was virtually superseded by that of St. Augustine. He formulates new theological ideals for the Western world for succeeding ages.

CHAPTER V

THE HUMAN SOUL

(i) Introduction

Philosophy, according to Augustine, may be defined as the "love of wisdom" ("amor sapientiae").[1] Wisdom is knowledge; it implies a diligent inquiry into those human and divine things that pertain to a happy life.[2] The highest object of all knowledge and investigation is God, and after God, comes the human soul. To know God and the human soul is not only Augustine's highest aspiration, but also his sole concern in life: "Deum et animam scire cupio. Nihilne plus? Nihil omnino."[3] He desires to know God because He is the Supreme Being.[4] He recognises within himself, moreover, an insatiable longing for perfect happiness; but reason tells him that this longing will be satisfied only when he enjoys God, Who is the Absolute Good.[5] He desires to know God, therefore, in order that he may one day enjoy Him and so attain perfect happiness.[6] He aspires to know the soul because it bears the image of God, and also because it is the medium through which he acquires a knowledge of God.[7] In these words we find the key to the understanding of his whole philosophy. All other problems group themselves naturally about these two focal points—God and the human soul. The study which pertains to the first and

[1] *Cont. Acad.*, ii, 3.
[2] *Cont. Acad.*, i, 8, 23.
[3] *Sol.* I, 2 vii.
[4] *De Civ. Dei*, xi, 20.
[5] *De Civ. Dei*, x, 6.
[6] *Ep.*, 118, 3.
[7] *Conf.*, x, 17.

more important of these two central ideas is of a theological rather than a philosophical character. The interest of the student of philosophy concentrates especially upon Augustine's concept of the human soul.

It is important to remember that Augustine did not formulate an acquired system of philosophy, which can be found in any one treatise or class of treatises; on the contrary, his philosophy is of a fragmentary nature and is diffused through his voluminous writings. Philosophical problems, as such, engross his attention only when they appear to be necessary to throw light on some difficult subject.

What is true of his philosophy, considered in this respect as a whole, applies also to that part of it which treats of the soul. A systematically developed, coherent, philosophical treatment of the soul is not to be found in the writings of St. Augustine. He did not investigate the origin and the nature of the soul as an isolated philosophical problem, but in connection with his theological expositions. This absence of a connected scientific treatment of the problem necessitates research in many directions to collect those principles which have been enunciated in different treatises.

The present day exponent of the reality of the soul, who finds himself face to face with the scepticism which is so evident amongst some students of biology and psychology, feels constrained, first of all, to formulate an answer to the question: "Does the human soul exist?" St. Augustine apparently was not called upon to contend with this particular aspect of the soul problem since, as he himself assures us, there is no one who questions the existence of the human soul. ("Quasi non evidentior sit in hominibus anima, quae utrum sit, nulla fit quaestio.")

It is remarkable that some of the basic arguments employed to-day in trying to prove the existence of the human soul can be found in the writings of Saint Augustine.

Every one who has even an imperfect acquaintance with the principal works of this great writer knows the importance he attaches to the introspective method of study ("Noli foras ire in te ipsum redi; in interiore homine habitat veritas").[1] He was endowed with a rare faculty of introspection, a remarkable talent for analysis, and the ability to record in expressive terms the results of his examination. As a matter of fact, he has been described as the founder of the introspective method.[2] As every student of the History of Philosophy knows, this is the original method of all psychology. Augustine was the first Christian philosopher to understand and to appreciate the scientific value of facts learned by this method.[3]

Augustine, unlike Aristotle and his Christian interpreter, Thomas Aquinas, did not begin by formulating a general theory of the soul, from which he passed by stages to consider different views of the human soul. There is no evidence to vindicate the assertion of Nourrisson that Augustine did not, in the first place, refer to the human soul, but commenced his investigation by asking himself —what is soul in general.[4] He adduces no evidence from the writings of St. Augustine to substantiate his assertion. After stating that Augustine, at the outset, considered the nature of the soul in general rather than the individual soul in particular, the French scholar admits that his

[1] *De Vera Relig.*, 39, 72.
[2] *Cath. Ency.* XIV, p. 155, art. *Soul.*
[3] Gonzalez-Pascal. *Histoire de la Philosophie* II, p. 89. Paris. 1890.
[4] *Philosophie de Saint Augustin*, p. 166. Paris. 1865.

interest certainly centred in the latter. In another passage of the same book, Nourrisson asserts that Augustine's theory of the soul was formulated in imitation of the teaching of Aristotle.[1] He makes no attempt, however, to prove this statement. We do not know definitely the extent of Augustine's acquaintance with the philosophy of Aristotle, neither can we say that he was familiar with his "De Anima," as we have no proof that it had been translated into Latin in Augustine's lifetime. We may also mention that Augustine was by preference a Platonist rather than an Aristotelian.

All the evidence we can obtain points to the fact that the human soul was for Augustine the starting point as well as the end of his investigation of the problem of the individual soul. Although he has something to say about the soul in general, and also refers to the plant soul, the world soul, and the animal soul, he makes these animadversions merely to explain in a more satisfactory way his main theme, which is that the knowledge of the human soul is second in importance only to understanding all that pertains to the Supreme Being. In the *Soliloquies*, the *De Immortalitate Animae*, and the *De Quantitate Animae*, the first three treatises, in which he deals, at any length, with the problem of the soul, there is no mention whatever of a general theory. On the contrary, in the first book of the *Soliloquies*, he declares expressly that he is interested only in the human soul. There can be no doubt about the object of his study in *De Immortalitate Animae*, inasmuch as he bases his most convincing proof of immortality on the reasoning faculty, which he believes to belong to man alone among terrestial creatures.[2] In

[1] P. 308.
[2] Ch. ii.

the treatise *De Quantitate Animae*, he makes the following explicit statement, which places the matter beyond all doubt: "In primis tamen tibi amputem latissimam quamdam et infinitam expectationem, ne me de omni anima dicturum putes, sed tantum de humana, quam solam curare debemus, si nobismetipsis curae sumus."[1]

Augustine's conception of philosophy may be summed up as follows: There is a philosophy of St. Augustine, but it is one of a religious nature. He desires to know only God and the human soul. He desires to know God for His own sake ; the soul for the sake of knowing God. His study of the soul is not purely a philosophical or psychological study; it is also a religious study. It is the soul of man and not the soul in general that chiefly engages his attention.[2]

It is important to collect and co-ordinate the philosophical fragments of St. Augustine's doctrine of the human soul and to interpret these in the light of his mental development. There is a tendency on the part of some writers to over-emphasise the Platonic character of Augustine's doctrine of the human soul. It is true that those treatises which were published during the first few years of his career manifest the great influence of his recent study of Neo-Platonism. The treatises, however, which belong to the period when he was Bishop of Hippo and one of the most renowned scholars of his day, stamp him unquestionably as a Christian philosopher. It is indispensable to the correct understanding of Augustine's concept of the human soul that due attention must be paid to the development which characterises his doctrine.

[1] Ch. xxxiii, 70.
[2] O'Connor. *Concept of the Human Soul*, p. 30.

(ii) The Origin of the Soul

The problem of the origin of the human soul as it is found in the writings of St. Augustine presents a two-fold aspect. There is, first of all, the fundamental question— does the soul come from God by creation? Secondly, there is the question of the time and manner of creation, which involves two distinct problems—how and when did the *first* human soul originate? How can the origin of *subsequent* souls be explained?

Augustine teaches very clearly that neither the soul of the first man, nor the souls of his descendants have been created by God in the sense that they have been engendered from His own substance; the human soul is not to be considered as emanating from the Creator as if in its essence it is divine.[1] At one time, Augustine appeared to think otherwise, because as he tells us,[2] he was then incapable of differentiating between the Divine Substance and the substance of the soul. When at a later time, he arrived at a clearer understanding of the nature of the Supreme Being, it became evident to him that it was impossible for a mutable substance, such as the human soul, to be identical with the absolutely unchangeable, incorruptible substance of God for, if it were, it could become neither better nor worse.[3]

He also warns his readers against believing that the soul of man was begotten from the substance of God as was His Divine Son, or that it came by way of procession as did the Holy Spirit, as if in its nature and substance it were identical with that of the Deity.[4]

[1] *De Gen. ad Litt.*, vii, 3, 4.;*De An. et ejus Orig.*, ii, 3; *Ep.*, 143, 7.
[2] *Conf.*, iv, 16.
[3] *Ep.*, 166, 2; *De Civ. Dei*, viii, 5.
[4] *De Gen. ad Litt.*, vii, 28.

The theory of the evolution of the soul is treated of by Augustine. He points out that no corporeal matter nor any irrational soul can be so transformed as to become a human soul.[1] If it were fashioned from corporeal matter, such as dust, of which God made Adam, or as the side of Adam, from which He made Eve, then, it follows logically, that the human soul must be corporeal—a conclusion which is contrary not only to known facts, but also to the teaching of the Catholic Faith.[2]

Therefore it follows that God either fashioned it from some already existing spiritual substance, or that He created it from nothing.[3] Augustine's own opinion was that the soul of the first man was created "ex nihilo."[4] The soul of the first woman also was created from nothing since the first woman was not an offspring of the first man by natural generation; her soul, therefore, was not descended from Adam, but was created "ex nihilo" by God.[5]

Concerning the time of origin of the first soul, he teaches that the soul is not eternal and that it did not previously exist in the sense expounded by Plato and Origen. He is certain that nothing created is co-eternal with the Creator.[6] He condemns the doctrine of the Pre-existence, as advocated by Pythagoras, Plato, and Origen,[7] in the name of Reason.[8] He realises that it is incompatible with Divine goodness to maintain that the

[1] De Gen. ad Litt., x, 4.
[2] De Gen. ad Litt., vii, 9.
[3] De Gen. ad Litt., x, 4.
[4] De Gen. ad Litt., x, 6, 7.
[5] Ibid, 10.
[6] De Civ. Dei, xii, 17.
[7] Ep., 155, 1.
[8] De An. et ejus Origine, iii, 7.

soul is united to the body in the present life in consequence of faults committed in some previous state of existence, for if it were true, Creation would be a punishment and not a blessing.[1]

As to the time when the first soul was created, Augustine could not draw any definite conclusion. He makes two suggestions: either the soul was created in the beginning, when "He that liveth for ever created all things together"; or it was created on the sixth day, at the moment of its union with the body.[2] He considers the former suggestion to be "credibilius et tolerabilius."[3] As to the latter suggestion, that it entered the body on the sixth day through direct Divine intervention or in some spontaneous manner, he is unable to arrive at any clear decision.[4]

Whatever the origin of the soul, it is not inferior to the stars or to the angels, no matter how exalted is their habitation. They are exalted beings who have never sinned. The human soul has sunk through sin to an inferior level, but, as to its nature, it is not inferior to the angels, though in function unequal ("Et illis superioribus officio quidem impares, sed natura pares").[5] As for the stars, Plato thought that they were souls of a high order, but Augustine regards them as corporeal in so far as relates to their light which bodily eyes can see.[6]

A question which was much debated in the Church of the early fifth century concerned the origin of the souls

---

[1] Ep., 156, 9; De Civ. Dei, xii, 26.
[2] De Civ. Dei, xii, 23.
[3] De Gen. ad Litt., vii, 24.
[4] De Gen. ad Litt., vii, 25–27.
[5] De Lib. Arbit., iii, 2, 32.
[6] De Lib. Arbit., iii, 9, 25.

of the descendants of the first man. This question engaged the attention of St. Augustine at frequent intervals during his career. We discover reference to it first in *De Libero Arbitrio*, written about A.D. 395. It receives further treatment in *De Genesi ad Litteram* and in several of his Epistles written between A.D. 401–418. It received special treatment in the treatise *De Anima et ejus Origine* about A.D. 420. When he wrote the *Retractations*, about A.D. 427, the problem was still unsolved, and in his last work, *Opus imperfectum contra Julianum*, written about A.D. 430, he still expressed his inability to arrive at a decision about the matter.

Augustine offers four hypotheses in regard to the origin of the soul: (1) Every soul is derived from the soul of the first man, through the generative act of the parents, the soul of Adam alone having been created. This was the theory held by Tertullian, Apollinaris, and the greater part of the Western Church. (2) God creates a special soul for each individual body in which it is incorporated. (3) All souls were created apart from their bodies at the beginning of the world and continue to exist in a kind of Divine treasury or reservoir of soul life, from which they are sent, as required, to inhabit a newly-created body. Augustine favours this last theory, and thinks that it is more in keeping with the fact that God rested after the Creation. It appears, however, that his theory throws the responsibility upon God in thus leaving the soul in ignorance and infirmity in its new state. As God makes the choice, every soul has not the same chance. (4) The soul descends into a body of its own accord.

Augustine states that, in offering these four explanations, his object is to treat them in such a way that, whichever of the four theories may be true, it would in no way be a handicap to him in contending with all his might against those who were attempting to make God the author of evil and sin.[1]

After careful examination of these four theories, it will be seen that they are reducible to two which are usually designated Creationism and Traducianism. The ablest advocate of Creationism in the time of Augustine was Jerome who, arguing from our Lord's words: "My Father worketh hitherto," supported the view that every soul that comes into being is produced by a special creative act of God. Jerome, commenting on Eccles., xii, 7[2] writes: "Hereby they are convinced of folly who think that souls are transmitted with bodies, and do not come from God, but are generated from the bodies of their parents." This theory was also supported by Optatus, an African Bishop.

Jerome, however, appears to be unwilling to state what he really believed on the subject, and refers inquirers to Augustine. The latter refuses to decide between the rival theories, although he discusses them at some length in several of his works. He also wrote a letter about the year A.D. 415, in which he gives a complete statement of the Creationist theory as he understood it.[3] This letter was forwarded to Jerome, but he never replied to it.

It will be remembered that, at the time of Augustine's writing this Epistle to Jerome, the problem of original sin was prominent in connection with the Pelagian controversy. This question of original sin was closely related to that of the Origin of the Soul. If the soul of each

[1] *Ep.*, 166, 7; *cf. De Lib. Arb.*, iii, 21.
[2] *Works*, III, 493.
[3] *Ep.*, 166.

born child was newly created, then the body alone was infected but not the spiritual nature, for how could a newly created soul be contaminated by moral evil with which it was in no way connected?

As regards the opinion held by Jerome, Augustine says that he is willing to adopt it, if he can be convinced that it is true and in perfect harmony with all the teachings of the Church. Some of the difficulties which others have raised are no stumbling block to him, but he has difficulties of his own, and these he is unable to solve. How does Jerome's theory explain the transmission of original sin and, at the same time, uphold the goodness and justice of God? He writes: "I inquire, therefore, about the ground of this condemnation of little children because, if souls are separately created, I do not admit that any of them sin at that age, nor do I believe that any one is condemned by God, whom He sees to have no sin."

If one should reply that sin is contracted by the mere fact that the soul is united to bodily members which are derived from another, how it is compatible with Divine justice that the infant be condemned to eternal punishment in case he should die without having participated in the grace of Jesus Christ by means of the sacrament of regeneration, since it does not lie within his power to procure this sacrament by his own efforts? Or again, in the case of an illegitimate birth, does God create a soul in response to human sin? Finally, if one accepts this theory, how does he explain the great diversity of talents in different souls, and how does he explain the unfortunate condition of those who come into the world absolutely devoid of reason?[1]

[1] *Ep.*, 166, 6.

Augustine's letter to Jerome remained unanswered, and the difficulties of Creationism remained unsolved; he knew no other means whereby the souls of infants might be cleansed from their original sin except by the Sacrament of Baptism.

The problem of the Origin of the Soul is considered in another letter of Augustine[1] addressed to Bishop Optatus. Pelagius argued that each soul is a separate creation and the body alone is derived from Adam. Augustine therefore asks: How could the soul be condemned by the mere entrance into the body? If, however, the soul is transmitted to the child from its parents, how can it be responsible for another person's sin?

Augustine points out that nothing can be ascertained from Scripture concerning the origin of individual souls. He declined to dogmatise, but he is evidently more inclined to believe that each soul is transmitted rather than a fresh creation. He justifies his own hesitation and uncertainty by quoting St. Paul's words expressing doubt as to whether he was in the body or out of the body when he was carried up to the third heaven.

Although it may be said that Augustine appears to lean to the side of Traducianism, yet the theory itself seems to lend itself to a materialistic conception of the soul.[2] A sense of fear, it may be mentioned, together with the belief that this theory attributes too much importance to secondary causes in the production of the soul, operated in subsequent times to dissuade theologians from giving sanction to the same hypothesis.

In *De Gen. ad Litt.*, vii, 35, 36, Augustine discusses the theory of the reservoir of soul life with a certain degree

---

[1] Letter 190.
[2] Cf. *De Gen. ad Litt.*, x, 40.

of sympathy, especially the idea that the soul finds its way into the body by a kind of natural tendency. This theory was doubtless commended to him by his Neo-Platonic studies.

It may be pointed out that Traducianism, in general, maintains that the soul of man is transmitted to the off-spring in the generative act of the parents, and, therefore, through human agency. When the term Traducianism is employed in a specific sense it implies that the soul is propagated by means of a material germ. This is some-times referred to as Corporeal or Materialistic Traducian-ism. This theory had been defended by Tertullian previously but was condemned by Augustine.[1] The other aspect of Traducianism, which teaches that subsequent souls descend from the soul of the first man through the parents, is frequently designated "Generationism."[2] Although Augustine was in a state of doubt and hesitancy in reference to the problem of the origin of the soul, yet, on the whole, he seems to have been inclined to favour this particular theory of Generationism.[3]

His chief reasons for favouring this view are given in different treatises. It safeguards the goodness and the justice of God by furnishing an adequate explanation of the penal sufferings of infants both here and hereafter[4]; it explains the transmission of original sin ("si una anima facta est, ex qua omnium hominum animae trahuntur nascentium, quis potest dicere non se pecasse, cum primus ille peccavit").[5] and his explanation, also, seems

[1] *De Gen. ad Litt.*, x, 24.

[2] *Cf.* Art. "Traducianism." C. A. Dubray. *Cath. Ency.*, xv, p. 14.

[3] See Beausobre. *Histoire critique de Manichée et du Manichaeisme.* Amsterdam. 1734.

[4] *Ep.*, 166, 4.

[5] *De Lib. Arb.*, iii, 20.

to be more in harmony with the teaching of the orthodox faith than the others.[1]

Although, as has been pointed out, Augustine favours the doctrine of Generationism, yet he does not fail to see the difficulty which arises in so far as the soul of Jesus Christ is concerned. If we adopt this theory, we must hold either that the soul of Christ, as an exceptional case, was not derived in the same way as the souls of other human beings, but came into existence through an act of special creation, or, if it were derived in the same way as the souls of other men, we must believe that when Christ assumed it, He so purified it that He came into the world sinless.[2]

Although the mind of Augustine sought untiringly, with the aid of both past and contemporary philosophy and of theology, for some solution of this problem which would harmonise with the orthodox doctrine of original sin, yet he was forced finally to acknowledge in the end of his days that so far as he was concerned the origin of the soul of the descendants of the first man is a profound mystery.[3]

We cannot refrain from expressing our admiration of the high quality of mind that prompted this great man to confess frankly that he did not know how to solve this difficulty, and, furthermore, was not ashamed to admit that he did not know ("Nunc autem nescio nec me pudet ut istum fateri nescire quod nescio").[4] He states that he had been beset by inquirers, but had been unable to solve their queries. Neither by prayer, reading, reflection, nor

[1] *Ep.*, 190, 1; *Ep.*, 202, 6.
[2] *Ep.*, 164, 7.
[3] *Op. Imp. cont. Jul.* II, 68.
[4] *De An. et ejus Orig.*, i, 15.

reasoning ("Neque cogitando et ratiocinando") had he been able to find a solution to the problem.[1] He is able, however, to limit the field of inquiry in which the truth is to be found, and is able to point out the weakness of many theories.

"This honest and open recognition of his intellectual limitations tends only to bring out in clearer perspective the rare quality of Augustine's genius. The great care and sustained effort devoted to this problem, combined with that critical attitude of mind, so indispensable in the searcher after truth, manifest to us how deservedly Augustine merits the title of 'Philosopher,' and lend an added sanction to the unanimous verdict of the ages which ranks him among the few really great thinkers of all times."[2]

(iii) Nature of the Soul

Augustine does not employ consistently technical language in his description of the soul and the mind. *Anima* means usually the vital principle of man as stirred by desire and love; *Animus* is the highest grade of Anima, that is, the soul as the principle of thinking. Of the *Intellectus* he says: "And so in our soul there is something called the intellect. This part of the soul which is called "intellectus et mens" is enlightened by a higher light. Now that higher light whereby the human mind is enlightened is God."[3] *Ratio*, on the other hand, is "the Movement of the Mind" ("Mens") which is capable of distinguishing and interrelating what is learnt."[4] The

---

[1] *Ep.*, 65, 4; *cf.* also *Ep.*, 143, 5, 6.
[2] O'Connor. *Concept of the Human Soul*, p. 75.
[3] In *Joh. Tract*, xv, iv.
[4] *De Ordine*, ii, 2, 30.

"Mens," however, is distinguished into a higher and lower activity, according as it is engaged on contemplation or action.

These distinctions are not inconsistent with the unity and substantiality of the soul. As a spiritual being, the soul is indivisible,[1] and its spirituality and subsistence are apprehended directly by self-knowledge. The soul knows, certainly, what it is, for it thinks "sum, si fallor."[2] The soul is conscious that it lives, that it remembers, that it knows, and that it desires. It recognises all this within itself.[3] Not that the soul needs or can possess all this knowledge at all times with full awareness, nor is it necessary to suppose that the soul comprehends its nature fully. In a sense it must do so, as it cannot know itself in part; and yet, since it is still searching for knowledge, it is unable to enjoy it completely.

Augustine insists so strongly on the spirituality and substantiality of the soul that he experiences a difficulty when he attempts to explain the soul's relation to the body. His language is very guarded and somewhat indefinite. "The manner in which spirits are united to bodies . . . is all together wonderful, and it transcends the understanding of man."[4] He is a little more definite in another passage: "The soul is a rational substance suitable to rule the body."[5] This definition is somewhat similar to that of the Neo-Platonist writers. Elsewhere Augustine says: "The soul is simple in its essence, but

[1] De Quant. Anim., xiv.
[2] De Civ. Dei, xi, 26.
[3] De Ord., ii, 2, 30.
[4] De Civ. Dei, xxi, 10.
[5] De Quant. Anim., i, 13.

manifold in its operations."[1] He also states: "Man is a rational soul using a mortal and earthly body." Man is one being and the soul vitalises the body, regulates its movements, and is present in every part by means of what he calls "attentio vitalis." In other words, the soul is an intermediary between matter and supreme spirit. "Nor can anything be discovered between the highest life and the body, save the soul which quickens it."[2]

The body is, indeed, the instrument of the soul, and the soul is the life of the body. The soul, however, is not only present in the body regarded in its entirety; but it is, at the same time, altogether present in each part of the body.[3] It is, therefore, an internal force, an incorporeal vital principle in the body.

According to Augustine's conception, God and the soul are, in a sense, bound together. "Deum et animam scire cupio. Nihilne plus? Nihil omnino."[4] It was not mere scientific curiosity that urged him to investigate the soul's nature. Modern psychologists probe into the soul's hidden recesses in a manner similar to that of the geologist who digs into the bowels of the earth, but Augustine's discussions on the soul are wafted on the wings of angels; they all soar upwards and scarcely ever descend to earth. The questions he considers in reference to this subject are the soul's immortality, its incorporeal nature, and similar problems.

It is noticeable that Augustine, when discussing this subject, does not introduce the names either of those who support or of those who oppose his teaching, even those

---

[1] *De Trin.*, iii, 2.
[2] *De Civ. Dei*, xi, 23.
[3] *De Fide et Symb.*, i, 10.
[4] *Solil.* i, 2.

of such great writers as Plato or Plotinus. He is not engaged in a scientific inquiry, and the introduction of the names of authorities would appear to be almost profane. Consequently, in our effort to discover Augustine's ideas on the nature of the soul, we must rely on occasional expressions on the subject which appear in the course of his various discussions.

The union of the soul with God mentioned in the *Soliliquies* is not an isolated thought. In one of his prayers he says: "Noverim me, noverim te," as it is through his knowledge of self that Augustine hopes to know God, as far as is possible. In his treatise, *Contra Academicos*, i, 8, he says that a man must know himself before presuming to think he may know God.

Augustine does not confine his attention to the soul with its individual setting. There are, also, many references here and there to the *relation of the soul to the universe*.[1] But, even in this respect, his interest is bound up with other questions, such as the effect of sin and the misery which accompanies it, and also of the perfection of the universe as the handiwork of God.

In treating of the human soul, Augustine lays emphasis, first of all, upon *its incorporeal nature*. He teaches that the human soul is not a body but a spirit. This is a doctrine on which his teaching never varied. He is always anxious to defend the doctrine of the spirituality of the soul against the attacks of the materialistic philosophers of his day. He maintains that the soul of man is an incorporeal, spiritual substance.[2] The materialists of Augustine's day were unable to conceive of any substance as existing of which they could not form an

[1] *De Lib. Arbit.*, iii, 9; *De Immort. Anim.*, xv.
[2] *De Gen. ad Litt.*, vii, 28.

image. To them, only bodies were real things, and what was not corporeal was nothing; consequently, they concluded that the soul of man must be a corporeal substance.[1] According to Augustine, the crux of the problem depends upon the meaning assigned to the terms "corpus" and "substantia." If the term "corpus" is employed to designate that which is in some manner self-existent, then, the soul is a body because it is a substance.[2] If, however, the term "corpus" is employed to signify a measurable unity which is extended in space, so that one of its parts is greater, and another less, and the whole is greater than any of its parts, the soul is not a body, because it is a simple, extended entity which has neither length, breadth, nor thickness.[3] That Augustine understood the term "corpus" in this last-named sense is evident from his definition of "corpus"; "quidquid majoribus et minoribus suis partibus majora et minora spatia locorum obtinentibus constat."[4] By "substantia" he means a being capable of subsisting in and by itself; one which does not require a subject in which to inhere.[5] The terms "corpus" and "substantia," therefore, as understood by Augustine, are not convertible expressions. While every "corpus" is also a "substantia," the converse of this is not true, namely, that every "substantia" is a "corpus."

The human soul is not a "corpus," but it is a "substantia"—it is not spatially extended; it has no measurable dimensions; but it is a simple substance which is present

[1] *Ep.*, 166, 2; *De Trin.*, x, 7.
[2] *Ep.*, 166, 2.
[3] *De Trin.*, vi, 6; *De Immort. An.*, 16.
[4] *De Anima et ejus Orig.*, iv, 12.
[5] *De Quant. An.*, i, 2.

simultaneously not only in the whole body but also in each of its parts, "non modo universae moli corporis sui sed etiam unicuique particulae illius tota simul adest.[1] When the soul is spoken of as a "simple substance," the term "simple" is used in a relative not in an absolute sense. Strictly speaking, God alone is a simple substance, because He alone is unchangeable; in Him alone there is perfect identity of essence and attribute, "quoniam quod habet, hoc est."[2] If the soul is a simple substance, devoid of parts and expansion, in what manner may it be said to be present in the body which it animates? This is answered by Augustine when he asserts that the soul is present in the body, not spatially, but virtually and potentially, "non spatio loci ac temporis sed vi ac potentia."[3] Or, as he expresses the same idea in another place, the soul pervades the body, not quantitatively, but by a certain vital intension.[4]

Augustine illustrates this description of the soul's incorporeality by saying that if the body is pricked in any one place by a sharp instrument, the whole soul is aware of the contact as having taken place at that particular spot. Similarly, if contact is made at two spots simultaneously, the soul is aware of each one separately, and of both at the same time. Since the whole soul, and not merely part, experiences these sensations, the feeling must be wholly present in each part of the body at the same time, "tota singulis partibus simul adest quae tota simul sentit in singulis."[5] And since it pervades the body

[1] *De Immort. An.*, xvi.
[2] *De Civ. Dei*, xi, 10.
[3] *De Quan. Anim.*, xxxii.
[4] *Ep.*, 166, 11.
[5] *De Immort. An.*, xvi.

in this unextended manner, it must be an incorporeal substance.

In the treatise *De Anima et ejus Origine*[1] Augustine speaks of the images which are fashioned by the act of thinking and stored up in the depths of Memory, whence they are reproduced in some mysterious manner when we wish to recall the objects they represent. If the soul were a body, it could neither form these images nor retain them, since they are so numerous and often representative of very large objects. Therefore, there is no doubt that the soul is spiritual and not corporeal.

Modern psychologists tell us that since image means a conscious representation, the retention of images is but a metaphorical expression.[2] It is not the image that is retained, but the "disposition or aptitude" to recall it that remains after the image has disappeared.

Augustine appears to have held that *"Sense-Memory,"* as well as *"Intellectual Memory,"* is an incorporeal faculty.[3] He argues that the former is not a material faculty because, if it were, it could not contain images which are not bodies but only the likenesses of bodies. The latter must be incorporeal since it retains the immaterial, such as thoughts,[4] the explanations of the liberal arts,[5] the principles of mathematics,[6] and the notions of such affections of the soul as desire, joy, fear, and sorrow.[7] It appears that he did not always distinguish clearly between Memory and Imagination. He leaves no room

[1] iv, 17.
[2] C. Dubray. *Introductory Philosophy*, p. 84. New York. 1913.
[3] *De Gen. ad Litt.*, vii, 21; *De Civ. Dei*, viii, 5.
[4] *Conf.*, x, 8.
[5] *Conf.*, x, 9.
[6] *Conf.*, x, 12.
[7] *Conf.*, x, 9.

for doubt, however, that he considers at least some operations of Memory to be spiritual in character, and, hence, concludes logically that the soul of which Memory is a faculty is incorporeal and spiritual.

Augustine was convinced about the *non-corporeality* of the soul. It is a problem which colours the conception of the soul's nature and it is dealt with in the treatises *De Quantitate Animae.* Thimme[1] says of this treatise: "This dialogue gives the impression that he is already sure of his subject; he has not to wrestle with thoughts, but spins them out with a certain leisureliness." This conviction means much when we reflect upon the character of the pre-Augustinian psychology.

The teaching on the soul had been released from the dark cells of Materialism and had reached the stage of the Pneuma-theory, but to Augustine this teaching was materialistic. He remarked to his friend Euodius that pneuma was as corporeal as could be. It possessed length, breadth, and height as truly as any set of walls.

He asserts that the category of Quantity cannot really be applied to the soul but only to bodies. The soul has real being, although it has no dimensions. In this treatise, Augustine carries on a series of arguments with Euodius, and the latter admits that Justice, which does not possess the dimensions of length, breadth, and height, is a much nobler thing than a tree which possesses them. Euodius then argues that the soul may be looked upon as "pneuma," but Augustine replies that he can conceive the wind as a body. Augustine persuades his opponent to acknowledge the fact that the wind has the characteristics of a body. ("Quid hoc aere longius et latius et altius facile inveniri

[1] *Augustins geistige Entwickelung,* p. 140.

potest, quem commotum, ventum esse nunc abs te mihi persuasum est."[1]

After conceding that the wind has dimensions, Euodius next argues that the soul must be of the same size as the body that contains it. Stoicism, indeed, taught that the soul, being diffused through the body, occupies the same geometrical dimensions as the body itself.

It was for the purpose of disproving this theory that Augustine appealed to the phenomenon of *Memory*. He points out that memory is able to retain images of things corporeal, such as cities and lands, but the images are not corporeal. Since these images may be of huge tracts of country, the soul containing these memory images must be larger than the dimensions of the body.

Another argument, taken up by Augustine to prove that the soul has no dimensions, is one which is concerned with geometrical dimensions. Mind is capable of thinking out and retaining an ideal line which is pure length, but such a line does not exist outside the mind. Because the soul can retain representations of the figure of Geometry which are incorporeal, it must be itself incorporeal.

The arguments on this subject, however, are not all of a negative kind. In *De Quant. Anim.*, xiii, 22, Augustine gives a clear and oft-quoted definition "si autem definiri tibi animum vis, et ideo quaeris quid sit animus: facile respondeo. Nam mihi videtur esse substantia quaedam rationis particeps regendo corpore accomodata." The human soul, therefore, is a "substantia" participating in reason and adapted to governing the body. It cannot be resolved into simpler elements. It is also rational and this rational character is the source of its power.

This definition contains in germ the entire psychology

[1] Ch. iv.

of St. Augustine and has been reproduced, with various modifications, by many modern philosophers. The definition clearly applies to the human soul. When he teaches that the human soul is a "living substance," he means that it is capable of immediate and spontaneous motion; it is not moved by being acted upon from without, except in so far as its activity comes ultimately from God, but its motion is intrinsic to itself; it belongs to the very nature of its being.[1]

In *De Mor. Manich.*, ii, 2, it appears that substance is that which has being ("Itaque et nos jam novo nomine ab eo quod est esse, vocamus essentiam quam plerumque substantiam etiam nominamus; ita veteres haec nomina non habebant, pro essentia et substantia naturam vocabant.") In Augustine's estimate of values, body occupies a low place, but not the lowest. Body is not "nihil," it is not "inane." Empty space is all "inane," but there is less of what is "inane" where body is; but there is much we must call "inane" in the composition of body, and we can only assign relative being to it. Matter and Form must be distinguished; it is Form which gives body its share of being. In *De Lib. Arbit.*, ii, 20, Augustine appears to conclude that body is a combination of Form and "inane." He points out that Form, which all things possess, constitutes that which is good in them; the very least trace of Form is to be reckoned as good, and when all Form is subtracted there is nothingness (nihil) left. But even the Form contained in body is no true Form; for, if it were, body would be spirit (animus).[2] The true Form appears to be identical with the "Figures" of geometry, about which Augustine can only say that

[1] *De Div. Quaest.*, lxxxiii, 8.
[2] *Solil.*, ii, 18.

they are either in the Truth, or the Truth is in them. Truth (veritas) represents the highest stage of being, for God is "veritas." And, consequently, as true Form is in the Truth and Truth is in true Form, and the soul is in the Truth, it follows that the soul is in true Form, and has the same reality of being as "veritas," or, more correctly, partakes of this reality.

The soul is also a *vivifying principle*. It is that by which we live, and feel, and carry on the operations of intellectual life.

Augustine regards the substance of the soul as both Intensive and Dynamic in its nature. The dynamic nature of the soul is expressed in the statement that it is a "vis quaedam." ("Ea vero inter virtutes, quae appellatur animi magnitudo, ad nullum spatium, sed ad vim quamdam, id est potestatem potentiamque animi relato, recte intelligitur.")[1] The notion of growth cannot be applied to the soul, because that implies a purely quantitative conception; time produces the ripening of the congenital inherent forces of the soul: the soul-dynamic is moulded and shaped; potential energy becomes a true energy ready for application.

This conception is strengthened and illustrated by the theory of *the soul as Life*. It is a Platonic conception and is found throughout Augustine's earlier writings. Augustine held, as did Plotinus, that the soul is essentially and indissolubly connected with life; not merely that life is added or imparted to it in some way, but this dynamic principle "Vita" is of its very essence. This thought is no proof of immortality, for life, like light, may impart itself indefinitely, and yet, in the end, vanish from its theatre of existence or perish altogether.

[1] *De Quant. Anim.*, xvii.

The soul is also the source of *Movement*. This idea is essentially connected with the notion of the soul as Force. These properties are founded on "Substantia." There is no motion without substantia. The soul is living substance: it moves the body but is itself unmoved.[1]

The movement of the body by the soul appears in two different spheres; in the sphere of the soul, this movement is active. But, having passed over into the body, the same is transformed into a passive form; in the latter sphere it is subject to place and time, whereas in the former it partakes of neither. Its independence of time is demonstrated by the fact that an act of intention embraces in itself past, present, and future.

The abolition of time in reference to the activities of the soul is a proof for Augustine of the resistance of the mind to the influence of bodily changes. The logical conclusion follows that if the soul is far removed from all time distinctions, there is no longer room for mutation within it. Augustine, however, appears to hesitate to come to this conclusion and therefore does not say definitely that the soul is immutable, but simply that its implication in the movement of the body does not make it mutable.

Reason, also, is characteristic of the human soul. It sets man apart from, and above, all the rest of terrestial creation.[2]

The body of man is, in fact, regulated by a reasonable soul. Beasts do not possess that inner sense, which is conscience. There is, certainly, a great difference between men and animals. Augustine expresses the nature of this

[1] *De Immort. Anim.*, iii.
[2] *De Civ. Dei*, xii, 23.

difference, when he says: "Bestiae, vim sentiendi habent, non scientiam."[1]

Augustine also states that the soul is adapted to the governing of the body, although he confesses that the mode of union between the corporeal and the spiritual creatures in man is incomprehensible (omnino mirus est, nec comprehendi ab homine potest.")[2]

Man may be defined, according to Augustine, as a rational substance, consisting of soul and body ("Homo est substantia rationalis constans ex anima et corpore").[3] The body is governed by a rational soul which has been breathed into it. "Hoc corpus inspirata anima regit, eademque rationalis."[4] The whole corporeal part of man is under the dominion of the soul, to which it is related as a servant or instrument.[5] "Let us call that alone a body which has a soul which is mistress of itself."[6]

This relationship is not to be understood in the sense that the body is nothing more than an external aid or trapping of the soul, for the body is something that pertains to the very nature of man.[7] According to the testimony of our own nature, we know that there must be a union of soul and body to constitute the complete man.[8] It is folly for any one to try to separate the body from human nature.[9] This union of soul and body that

---

[1] De Quant. Anim., xxviii.

[2] De Civ. Dei, xxi, 10.

[3] De Trin., xv, 7.

[4] De Trin., iii, 2.

[5] De Civ. Dei, x, 6.

[6] De Mor. Eccl. Cath., i, 4.

[7] De Civ. Dei, i, 13.

[8] De Civ. Dei, x, 29.

[9] De An. et ejus Origine, iv, 2.

results in man is a personal union.[1] It is this union that distinguishes Augustine's doctrine from the exaggerated dualism of Plato, who regarded man as spirit joined to a body accidentally and guiding it after the manner of the charioteer directing his chariot. It is true that in his earlier writings Augustine employed a formula somewhat analogous to that of Plato,[2] which was due perhaps to his contact with the writings of the Neo-Platonists, but this view he set aside in later years for that referred to in *De Civitate Dei.*[3]

Augustine advances still further in his argument. He first asserts by means of a negative argument, that if the soul is not incorporeal, it could not comprehend anything incorporeal. He then proceeds from a positive standpoint, that since the soul of man is capable of perceiving incorporeal entities, it must itself be incorporeal, with an intensive quality. ("Oportet animam quo videmus illa incorporalia, corporeum corpusve non esse.") Such an entity is the Geometrical point. The soul is comparable to the Point, for it is without dimensions, and, according to the teaching of Geometry, cannot be cut; in fact it is incorporeal. Yet the geometrical point, although without magnitude is capable of possessing a certain Force ("puncti potentia").[4] He suggests that when ordinary objects are more devoid of size ("sine tumoribus"), the more Force they exhibit. The eye serves as an illustration. The pupil of the eye is a kind of point and is capable of taking in an extensive skyline at the same time. The smaller eye of the eagle is even more powerful, thus the

---

[1] *Ep.*, 137, 3.
[2] *De Moribus Ecclesiae Catholicae*, i, 27.
[3] *De Civ. Dei*, xv, 7.
[4] Ch. xii.

power of sight does not depend upon the magnitude of the pupil. Therefore, the soul, which is the seat of Ratio, although without magnitude, is yet real and not devoid of substance.

There can, however, be no doubt that Augustine has a clear consciousness of what may be called the meta-physical difficulty of the interrelation of spirit and matter, which had led so many modern psychologists to adopt some form of psycho-physical parallelism. Basing his argument on this inter-relation as a fact, he explains it as an "*a fortiori*" proof of the correctness of man's outlook in believing the Incarnation. In one of his letters to a pagan philosopher, who had raised certain difficulties about the Incarnation, he writes: "In the person of man there is a combination of soul and body. In the person of Christ there is union of the Godhead with the nature of man, that is to say, with a soul having a body. The union of two immaterial substances (God and soul) ought to be more easily believed than that in which one is immaterial and the other material."[1] Notwithstanding his recognition of the difficulties of this teaching, he boldly expresses his belief in the reciprocal influence of mind and body. We can imagine that the following words were written by a psychologist of modern times: "It is my opinion that every movement of the mind affects in some degree the body. This is patent even to the senses, when the move-ments of the mind are vehement, as in grief, anger, and so forth. Hence we may conjecture that, when we are thinking, although no bodily effect would be discernible by us, there may be some such effect which would be discernible by beings with higher perceptive faculties. Therefore these footprints of its influence which the

[1] *Ep.*, 137, 11.

mind impresses on the body, may, perchance not only remain but set up as it were a certain disposition."[1]

We cannot fail to recognise that he is not without a conception of the working of the soul in the body. We may pay a tribute to his acuteness of mind, and express it in modern terminology, by saying that he does not regard it as an explanation, but only as a description of the facts.

Augustine distinguishes also between sense knowledge and intellectual knowledge; the former is acquired through the medium of the senses; the latter through the operation of the mind itself.[2] He asserts that, in addition to the knowledge which is acquired through the instrumentality of the bodily faculties, there are many things we know, "incorporaliter atque intelligibiliter."[3] It is impossible, he points out, for philosophers to form images of Wisdom and Truth corresponding to these realities, and yet they must be present to the mind in some way, otherwise they could not be discussed. They know Wisdom and Truth, therefore, not as they know those things with which they come into contact by means of images, but, directly, by pure thought.[4]

This argument is interesting in view of the fact that the problem of "Imageless Thought" is receiving some attention at the present time in the field of Experimental Psychology. It is a remarkable fact that the same question, as to whether there can be any thought without its concomitant image, was mooted in Augustine's day.

In a letter written to Augustine about the year

[1] *Ep.*, ix, 3.
[2] *De Trin.*, ix, 3; *Ep.*, cxviii, 14.
[3] *Ep.*, cxviii, 14.
[4] *Ep.*, cxviii, 4; *De Gen. ad Litt.*, x, 24.

A.D. 389, Nebridius, a friend of his, had stated it as his opinion that there could be no thought without some kind of an image: a word-image at least must be present in every act of thinking.[1] Our author disagrees with this opinion and maintains that it is possible for us to think about certain things without any concomitant image. We are able to think of Eternity, for instance, without forming any image of it.[2] In several other writings similar instances are given, such as Faith, Hope, and Charity.[3] Ideas of this kind can be apprehended only by pure reason.[4] Since the soul of man is capable of apprehending the purely spiritual, Augustine logically infers that the soul must be an incorporeal, spiritual substance.[5]

Augustine also points out that the soul of man, although it is fashioned in the image and likeness of God is *not a part of God*.[6] Created by God, the soul is not God; it does not participate in the Divine substance, as the Manichaeans, Priscillianists, and Origenists maintained[7]; Augustine rejects this idea as heretical and even as a horrible blasphemy.[8] It is obvious that the soul is subject to change, and is, in a certain sense, corruptible; but, God is in every respect immutable and incorruptible; the soul, therefore, cannot be a part of God. Nevertheless, God is its dwelling place and its true native land.[9]

Again, the human soul is *not part of a universal soul*. It

[1] *Conf.*, ix, 3; *Ep.* vi.
[2] *Ep.*, vii.
[3] *De An. et ejus Orig.*, iv, 20.
[4] *Ep.*, 118, 3.
[5] *De An. et ejus Orig.*, iv, 14.
[6] *Ep.*, 166, 2.
[7] *De Civ. Dei*, xi, 22.
[8] *De An. et ejus Orig.*, ii, 2.
[9] *De Vera Relig.*, xliv.

is an individual entity. At one time, Augustine does not appear to have been certain as to whether there is a universal soul for all men or a particular soul for each individual.[1] At a later time, this doubt disappeared and he insists most emphatically on the individual character of the human soul.[2]

With regard to the *simplicity of the soul*, Siebert[3] asserts in reference to *De Trin.*, vi, 6, 8, that Augustine does not teach the doctrine of the absolute simplicity of the soul. In *Sol.*, ii, 1, in answer to the question: "Simplicem te sentis anne multiplicem?" he answers "Nescio," but in Augustine's earlier writings the doctrine of the simplicity of the soul is maintained.[4] He defends the doctrine of the simplicity of the soul by saying that we count earth and air as simple elements; much more should we believe the soul to be simple and not compound. Even in his treatise *De Trinitate*, the compound nature of the soul is taught only in a special sense; it is complex in view of the very different moods which it displays, such as desire, fear, joy, sorrow, etc. Each of these is something by itself, different from the others.

Certain arguments are refuted by Augustine. The first one is the assertion that the soul grows as the body develops. He emphasises that quality and quantity are two distinct things ("aliud esse quod majus, aliud quod malius").[5] A circle is superior to a square because there is a certain point within a circle, termed the centre, from which all lines drawn to the circumference are equal.

---

[1] *De Quan. An.*, xxxii, 69.
[2] *De Lib. Arb.*, ii, 9; x, 28.
[3] *Gesch. der Psychologie* I, *Teil* II, p. 385.
[4] *De Quant. Anim.*, iv.
[5] Ch. xvi, 27.

This quality is called "Aequalitas," and virtue is a kind of Aequalitas in human life. The change which takes place in a man's soul, as he grows older, may be likened to the change from a square to a circle and to the development of "aequalitas" within. A boy is not necessarily wiser in proportion to his height.

We must mention that the illustrations employed by Augustine are different from those used by Plotinus, and his treatment of the subject furnishes evidence of his own independent reasoning.

Augustine follows up the argument, suggested by Euodius, that if as the body grows with age, the soul at the same time gathers more and more power by asking, does not this suggest that the soul grows in proportion to the body?[1] Augustine employs an argument similar to that he brought forward when refuting the idea that growth of the soul is implied in learning. The increase of physical power does not solely, or principally consist of a mere accession to the amount of bodily strength, but in a certain conformation of the bodily members. Athletes are strong and agile, not in proportion to their size, but in proportion to the quality and condition of their muscles.

Although the law of gravitation is at work in the case of stones thrown from a height, yet in the case of living bodies, the mind which wills the movement, has a force different from that of dead bodies. The mind employs the nerves as a human catapult ("nervis quasi tormentis utitur") and thus creates force. If the soul grows, its increased dimensions would not affect its operations.

Augustine does not appear to be so satisfactory in his answer to the next argument. It has been suggested that

[1] Ch. xxi.

the diffusion of sensation throughout the whole body presupposes the equal extension in space of soul and body alike. He shows that bodily sensation does not necessarily imply the presence of the soul throughout every part of the body. The argument is not always clear. He argues that the soul is never passive as it always takes an active part in sensation and perception, for it allows nothing to escape it ("latere animam"). This statement of Augustine is not psychologically true. The more concentrated the act of attention, the narrower the focus of consciousness. Strong stimulation of sense perception may be necessary before the mind is made aware of sensation. In *De Musica*, vi, 8, it is seen that the term, "non latere animam" is equivalent to "sentire" and, accordingly, indicates an active process. The mind is said to become conscious of certain changes in the body condition and, for this purpose, it is not necessary that the soul should be present in all the extremities of the body. The soul like the eye, is active at the point where the object is, but it is not necessary for the soul to be present at the exact spot where the sensation takes place.

Augustine seems to imply at times that the soul need not be in the body at all. ("Nonne istis rationibus confici potest animas nostras non esse in corporibus.")[1], and then, with a desire to avoid further difficulties he suggests that Euodius should bring forward further objections.

The next objection refers to the movements of parts of an insect after dissection—a fact which suggests that the soul is contained in each separate section, and that the soul is thus divisible and consequently corporeal.

[1] *De Quant. Anim.*, xxx, 61.

It may be remarked that Aristotle uses the same illustration.[1]

Augustine appears to have been weak, psychologically, on the side of sensation. This was due, no doubt, to the lack in his day of psychological knowledge of the nervous system. Simple reflex explains the problem of the insects.

Augustine finds an answer in an analogy concerning words. This analogy, according to Woerter[2] is taken from Plato.[3] He points out that words are composed of two elements—sound and meaning, and these are quite distinct. They correspond to the body and the soul residing in it. It is possible to divide the word into letters, but in so doing the meaning is unaffected, but the sound of the word is lost. In some such way we may consider the case of soul and body.

The conclusion is summed up in Chapter xxxii: if we speak of the soul as having quantity, the expression is to be understood in a dynamic sense. "Nunc accipe a me, si voles, vel potius recognosce per me, quanta sit anima, non apitio loci ac temporis sed vi ac potentia."

The philosophical doctrine of Spiritualism as it is found in Christian philosophy received much of its development from St. Augustine. It is true that he borrowed freely both from the Pagan and from the Christian philosophers who preceded him, yet he deserves not a little credit for the admirable manner in which he synthesised the best elements of their teaching and brought them to a higher stage of development. He is the channel through which the spiritualistic findings

[1] Cf. De Anima i, 5; ii, 2.
[2] Die Unsterblichkeitslehre in den philosophischen Schriften Augustins. Freiburg. 1880. p. 52.
[3] Theaetetus, p. 203. ff.

of the past were transmitted to the Christian thinkers of subsequent times. Those who came after him in the great scholastic movement employed the arguments which he had collected, and both further developed and perfected them. Augustine's system of doctrine suffered from the want of a fixed, clearly defined and expressive terminology. This terminology was contributed by the Schoolmen and constituted a most useful addition to the Christian philosophy of the soul. The place which this problem occupies in Christian philosophy is important, because it rests upon the significant question of the immortality of the soul.[1]

(iv) Relation of Soul to Body

The great scholastic philosopher, Thomas Aquinas, attacked the teaching of Augustine that all body, of whatever kind, is inferior to the soul, and that light, which was regarded by Augustine as a body, even though it holds the first place among bodies, is yet inferior to the soul on account of its material nature. Thomas Aquinas, as the champion of the doctrine of Aristotle and in opposition to that of Plato, maintained that Augustine made the statement on the authority of the philosophy of the latter (Plato) to which he had listened as a student.[2]

Even in its degradation the soul does not lose its non-corporeal nature ("Anima, quae ad quantamlibet sui decoris diminutionem defectumque perveverit, omnium corporum dignitatem sine ulla dubitatione semper superabit")[3] and, in consequence, it is ever able to maintain its superiority.

[1] O'Connor. *Concept of the Human Soul*, p. 56.
[2] II *Sent*, 13.
[3] *De Lib. Arbit.*, xvi.

Such essential superiority is a guarantee of its integrity and force; for superior nature, according to a principle held firmly by Augustine, implies superior force also. Consequently, in the midst of all bodily changes, the soul continues unchanged. ("Miramur quippe animi naturam mutabilitate corporis non mutari.")

Pliny expressed surprise when he realised the influence of the body on the soul. St. Augustine, on the other hand, marvels that the soul, in spite of all bodily influences, should remain unchanged.

Soul and body are accordingly, in their nature essentially disparate.

It must be borne in mind, however, that many of his earlier views on the human soul, such as are expressed in *De Libero Arbitrio*, were modified and even radically changed in after years.

In reference to the disparity of the soul and body, Augustine says that virtues have their seat in the soul, and not in the body, and consequently the soul cannot be defiled by violence done to the body.   ("De pudicitia, vero, quis dubitaverit, quin ea sit in ipso animo constituta, quandoquidam virtus est, unde a violento stupratore eripi nec ipsa potest.")[1] Such a statement, we can well imagine, could on occasion be perverted in meaning and made an excuse for lewdness.

Augustine attacks three erroneous views of the relation of the soul to the body.

(1) That of Pythagoras who taught that the soul was a Harmony of the body. Augustine observes that a Harmony of the body must needs be inseparably connected with the body; it must be in the body and there can be nothing in this Harmony which is not likewise in the

[1] *De Lib. Arb.*, i, 5.

body itself. Now, body is mutable, and therefore Harmony must also be mutable. Ratio, however, which is neither the soul, nor is contained in it, is immutable, and therefore Ratio or the soul cannot be such a Harmony; in fact, the soul cannot be the Harmony of the body. Augustine accordingly dismisses this Pythagorean theory.

Plotinus, also, attacks this doctrine of the soul as Harmony. He recounts, in rapid succession, a number of arguments, entirely different from those of Augustine's; he says that the soul is the earlier existing harmony; the soul is stronger than the body and combats it, and this Harmony could not do; the soul is substance, but Harmony is no substance. Again, if the soul is itself Harmony, then a soul must be postulated as existing before it, in order to produce it, just as harmony from the strings of the instrument posits a musician.[1]

(2) The second theory which he attacks is that of the soul regarded as Temperatio; the arguments against it are similar to those directed against the theory of Harmonia; the argument, however, is somewhat more replete with detail. Temperatio and Harmonia appear to be only different expressions for the same theory, although Augustine does not appear to realise this. This suggestion may be accounted for by the fact that the two theories may have reached him from their original source along different channels. Augustine writes[2]: "ut nonnulli opinati sunt debemus credere." Temperatio is regarded as like form and colour, and these are not substances, but are inseparably connected with the body, although independent of it, and this would not be possible if it were Temperatio of the body.

[1] Parry. "*Augustine and Platonism,*" p. 9.
[2] De Immort. Anim., x.

Temperatio is, indeed, the proportional union of the four elements of which the body is composed.

(3) The third theory attacked is that of Aristotle. Here the attack is indirect. It may be termed "the soul considered as Entelecheia." Aristotle based his theory upon the movement of dissected insects. Augustine refers to this theory in *De Quant. Anim.*, and he finds it hard to neutralise the impression produced by his teaching.

Augustine is in agreement with Plato and Plotinus in his description of the precise relationship of the soul to the body. The former is the source of life for the latter. The soul occupies, according to Plato, a middle position between the real world of ideas and the world of appearance, to which the body belongs, and is the mediator and dispenser of life for the latter.

Augustine follows the teaching of Plato in this respect.

The soul is not only the source of life for the body, but also that by means of which body becomes for the first time an organised entity (*corpori speciem tradit*); the soul is the continuous support of the body.

In his earlier years Augustine appears to have believed in the Platonic *world-soul*, as well as in the individual soul; this world-soul is for the world of appearance what the individual soul is for the body.[1]

At a later time, while he does not positively reject this doctrine, he declares that it is hardly credible.[2] Finally in the *Retractationes*, he warns his readers against rashly embracing such a doctrine.[3]

He describes in detail the functions of the soul in

[1] *De Immort. Anim.*, xv.
[2] *De Civ. Dei*, x, 29.
[3] i, 5.

relation to the body when mentioning the soul's seven stages of development.[1] The soul vivifies the body, holds it together and keeps it from decay; it regulates the process of nutrition, it preserves proportion and form; it is active, also, in the realm of sensation; it also seeks what is advantageous for the body and rejects what is disadvantageous; it brings about, moreover, the union of the sexes, and sees also to the care and feeding of the unborn young. The soul is superior to the body, not because it is its artificer, but because it is rational.[2]

In reference to the diffusion of the soul through the body, Augustine upholds its *nonspatial character*, yet he assumes that the soul is locally placed within the body.[3] The nonspatial character of the soul, however, is a source of continual perplexity; if the soul is in the body, how can it contemplate within itself images of very large objects? How can such a soul be conceived of as diffused through every part of the body?[4]

If the soul is diffused through every part of the body, it is logical to believe in a growth of the soul corresponding to that of the body. This point is discussed by Augustine, and he refutes the notion of growth. The soul, nonspatial in character, is brought, as the result of its connection with the body into intimate connection with something spatial; the bond of union, however is non-spatial.[5]

It is impossible, therefore, that the element which mediates between soul and body at the last stage of perception and sensation, can be the medium of union.

---

[1] *De Quant. Anim.*, xxxiii.
[2] *De Ordine*, ii, 19.
[3] *De Quant. Anim.*, v, 7.
[4] *De Quant. Anim.*, xv, 26.
[5] *De Immort. Anim.*, xvi.

Light, although of such an ethereal and apparently immaterial nature, is in reality material in character. But no material thing can form the bond of union or meeting-point of body and soul; the union is consummated from above, rather than from below.

By means of "Rationes," body and soul are united together. Here is the factor common to both, although they differ greatly in the degree of their participation. This difference is measured by the superiority of the mind to the body; the mind is essentially of the same nature as the "Rationes," viz. eternal and unchangeable. In this theory there appears to be some approach to Aristotelian teaching which aims at bringing body and soul together, and thus represents the perfection and consummation of the one as found in the other.

Material things and the soul differ in their behaviour as regards space. Material things (moles) can only extend by diffusion—parts are present in parts—but the soul can be present in its entirety in the part.

This theory is proved by the fact that the whole soul is conscious of an affection in any particular part of the body which it can quite distinctly locate in that part, without confusion with the sensations of the whole body; in the case of an injury to the foot the other parts of the body are set in motion, the eye moves, the mouth speaks, and the hand makes a movement. This will not take place unless the soul which is present in those different parts is also present in its entirety in the foot. The intervening parts act as message carriers from the one to the other until the terminus is reached; but the whole soul is present in each part.[1]

In accordance with his definite principle of the

[1] Parry. "Augustine and Platonism," p. 12.

superiority of the soul to the body, Augustine never admits that the soul adopts a passive role. It is not difficult to believe in the active relation of the soul to the body, but there are certain aspects of the theory which present difficulties. Augustine endeavours to overcome these difficulties.

The relation of the soul to the body in sensation ultimately necessitates a view of the soul as passive, but he makes an attempt to preserve the dignity of the soul by formulating a special theory of sensation. Sensation is "non latere animam quod corpus patitur." It implies the soul's active participation in sensation; the fact of sensation evidences the soul's watchfulness, and that is an active quality.

In *De Musica*, vi Augustine seeks to explain how the expression "non latere animam," referred to in *De Quantitate Animae*, is to be understood. He supposes that a fine material substance acts as mediator between the soul and the body in the processes of sensation and perception. This fine material substance appears to fulfil the function of the nervous system, as now understood. An effect produced in the body from outside, e.g. a blow, is transmitted to this fine substance where it produces a disturbance. Travelling still, it finally reaches the soul; the soul, however, far from being passively affected, takes active notice of it—"non latere animam."

Later, he seems definitely to regard this finest of material substances to be fire, light, or air.[1] The idea of light as the medium between body and soul is a Plotinian thought, and through the writings of Augustine it has become known to Christian philosophers. Thomas Aquinas agrees with Augustine that the grosser parts of

[1] *De Gen. ad Litt.*, vii, 15.

the body are moved by the finer parts and that the *first* species of this motive power is a kind of spirit.

The quality of a sensation, whether it be pleasurable or painful, depends upon the nature of its effect upon the body's processes. The fine material medium assumes a different form, according to the senses with which it is concerned; its form is "light-like" to the eyes, mobile and airlike to the ears, mistlike to the nostrils, damp to the mouth, and for the sense of touch, it is earthy. In all these operations Augustine is convinced that the soul evidences its activity.[1]

He gives further details about the nature of *Hearing*. The ears, he says, are a sensitive membrane; in that membrane is the airlike element already referred to, and the percussion of the exterior air acts upon this element in the membrane. The soul is perpetually engaged in imparting life to the ears, and this it does quietly and un-noticed; but when a sound is made, this soul sets in motion the air around the organ, the movement of which preceded the entrance of sound into the ears. In all this the soul plays a purely active part.

Augustine's description of the relation of the soul to the body brings to mind the teaching of Plotinus, although the latter is more moderate in his views than the former. Augustine first determines that a passive role cannot be assigned to the soul, and modern psychological teaching proves that he was right in assigning an active role to the mind in sensation, and thus there was no real necessity for him to strive with the courage of despair to defend his thesis.

Augustine connects the subject of *Sleep and Dreams* with that of the soul, for he insists that, although the soul,

[1] *De Musica*, vi, 5.

apparently, rests in a state of sleep, a helpless prisoner within the body, it is not so in reality. Neither by sleep nor by any sensation is the influence of the soul diminished. Sleep comes to us chiefly as a welcome and invited guest, but not always.

Sometimes it involuntarily takes the soul unawares. Sleep, however, is a characteristic simply of the body and the senses. It soothes the senses of the body, and the mind yields to its influence with pleasure. It refreshes the body after its labours, yet it does not deprive the mind of its power of perception or understanding; for even in sleep there are present to the mind images of things of sense, which are so realistic as to be indistinguishable from realities. The body alone and not the soul is confined in fetters by sleep. Even a discussion may be carried on in sleep by which we may learn something. Circumstantial details, such as the place of the discussion and the person with whom we disputed may deceive, but these are only the husk, which time, like a wind, carries with it into the oblivion of the past, yet much that is of value may remain. All this proves that, although the body may be lethargic, yet the soul is unconquerable.[1]

(v) The Immortality of the Soul

The immortality of the soul, according to Augustine, means that the soul is of such a nature that it will live always; that, although it is created in time, it will not perish in time;[2] that it is not absolutely undying as is God, but it is immortal in a manner peculiar to itself.[3]

Augustine, in two of his treatises, attempts to offer a

---

[1] De Immort. Anim., xiv; Cont. Acad., iii, 11.
[2] De Civ. Dei, xi, 4.
[3] Ep., 143, 7.

proof of the immortality of the soul. Book i of the *Soliloquies* is devoted to this theme, and it also constitutes the subject of the entire treatise *De Immortalitate Animae*. Both of these books were written about the year 387. The central pillar upon which the whole burden of the proof rests is the essential relationship between the soul which knows and the Truth which is known.

Attempting to define Veritas, Augustine draws a distinction between this term and "verum." He points out that nothing can be true (verum) except in and through the Truth itself. As "veritas" is immortal, a true thing (verum) is immortal. His inference is, that only immortal things are true, and no perishable object has true existence. Because truth is immortal, therefore the soul is immortal. In this way Augustine has been led along the path of logic to the direct teaching of Platonism.

In *Sol.*, book ii, Augustine again treats of the subject from the point of view of experience elicited through the problem of Ratio, or Reason, personified for the sake of the discussion. Augustine appears to have failed to connect this experience with the conclusions already obtained. Thimme has noticed this apparent omission, but he overlooks the fact that Augustine had not yet advanced so far in his thinking. He was not yet sure of his own true thinking existence. He had not yet joined together the ideas of thought and life so as to arrive at the idea of intelligent being. In a word he had not arrived at the Cartesian principle "Cogito ergo sum." Several other writers have discussed this passage, including Woerter, Ritter, and Matinée.

The argument proceeds, and the question arises whether anything true can exist, if truth does not exist? If we assume that this is impossible, it follows that if the world perished, truth would still exist, for it would be true that the world perished. Truth cannot perish.

In order to acquire a better knowledge of Truth, the nature of its opposite, Falsitas, is investigated. Since deception depends upon wrong assent, the source of error is concluded to be in the mind and not in the object.

The first thesis, which Augustine postulates, is that Falsity depends upon the existence of a person to whom a statement appears to be false. What appears, appears to the senses, therefore falseness depends upon the senses. This implies a soul behind them, therefore falseness posits the soul.

The difficulty of discovering truth proves the existence of falseness and those who are alive can only conceive that the soul exists. This statement cannot be termed a satisfactory proof of the immortality of the soul; we may say that it is a kind of proof that the soul exists as long as falseness exists. Even Augustine appears to recognise the insufficiency of the argument to prove immortality.[1]

Additional definitions of falsitas are given. "False is that which is different from that it appears to be, and true is that which is what it appears to be." Another definition follows: "False is that which imagines itself to be what it is not, or being non-existent strives to be." ("Falsum est quod aut se fingit esse quod non est, aut omnino tendit esse et non est.")[2]

When treating of what is false, Augustine considers it necessary to explain the difference between "falsum," "fallax" and "mendax." The existence of what is false makes a continued mental activity necessary in order to

[1] Parry. "*Augustine and Platonism*," p. 50.
[2] *Sol.*, ii, 9, 16.

distinguish it rightly. The continued activity of the mind implies the perpetual existence of the mind itself.

Another proof has thus been furnished. This proof is a link in a further proof. Imitatio is a fact in the world. Falsitas serves as the foundation of Imitatio. The latter is ever trying to enter into the region of Truth and must be carefully watched and detected. This suggests the function of the "Disciplinae" as special sciences. In these the mind is at work detecting Falsitas, and putting it into its own proper category. The Disciplinae are the guardians and revealers of truth, They are thus connected with Veritas.

Augustine next seeks to find a connection between the Disciplinae and the Mind, for since Veritas is immortal, so the Mind must be immortal. The proof is applied by means of a further principle: "Omne quod in subjecto est, si semper manet, ipsum etiam subjectum maneat semper necesse est."[1] From this it follows that as Truth is immortal, and through the Disciplinae is essentially connected with the mind, therefore is the mind immortal.

Augustine appears to be satisfied with the proofs he has brought forth, and triumphantly writes: "Jamque crede rationibus tuis, crede veritati. Clamat et in te esse, habitate et immortalem esse, nec sibi suam sedem quacumque corporis morte posse subduci."

Thimme believes that the *De Immortalitate Animae* is an advance on the *Soliloquiae* in that the former treatise distinguishes clearly between Veritas and Disciplina-Ars, placing Ratio between them; but it will be observed that in *Soliloquia* ii, Augustine distinguishes between Veritas and the Disciplinae, although he does not always evidence

[1] *Sol.*, ii, 24.

consistency.[1] There is no question raised concerning the relative superiority of Ratio and Disciplina, as Thimme seems to suggest, but the superiority of Ratio over the body is the question discussed.[2]

Another proof rests upon the relation of the soul and body, respectively, to Movement. The relation between the two is one of moving and being moved. That which is being moved is liable to perish, but the soul, as the moving agent, is not liable to such danger. The activity of the mind, although taking place in time and place as regards its effects, is itself above time and place; its acts involve past, present, and future in the one movement, and thus its real independent nature is demonstrated. It is then eternal in its nature and above change.

Augustine tries repeatedly to prove that the soul will not only continue to exist after death, but will have perpetual life. ("Animo etiam vita sempiterna maneat necesse est.")

In basing his doctrine of the immortality of the soul, chiefly, upon the eternal nature of veritas and its essential indwelling in the soul, the teaching of Augustine resembles in certain particulars the arguments of Plato and Plotinus. This fact has been stressed, perhaps unduly, by Woerter, who finds reminiscences of these two writers in Augustine's attacks upon the objections to the theory of immortality. It must be mentioned, however, that every argument is transformed when it proceeds from Augustine's mind. There are evidences of Augustine's independent mental attitude, for instance, in his treatment of memory.

The intellectual character of the soul, also, receives

[1] See Parry. *Augustine and Platonism*, p. 53.
[2] *De Lib. Arb.*, i, 1.

original treatment in the work of Augustine. Plotinus, for instance, argues that since the soul is divine and eternal, because of its incorporeal nature, therefore the soul is good and intellectual in nature,[1] and is thus qualified to acquire knowledge of the truth. Augustine, however, carries the inquiry a stage further and using this conclusion as the promise for a further argument, deduces therefrom (as we have seen) the immortality of the soul.

The chief proof of the immortality of the soul used by Plato in the *Phaedo* is the connection of the soul with the world of Real Ideas. The real sphere of the soul is not in the place to which it has been usually assigned, in the midst of the world of sense perceptions. In the world of Real Ideas, it attains to peace and clearness. This is a proof of kinship between the soul and this real world. Like the eternal ideas, the soul is also eternal and changeless. This view implies the theory of the pre-existence of the soul. According to Augustine and Plato, the soul does not ascend to the highest position. The soul is not "summa vita."

Although there are many reminiscences of Plotinus in the writings of Augustine, yet he is by no means guilty of having servilely copied his statements. Differences of ideas and of style strengthen this conclusion. Referring to this comparison Thimme observes that Augustine draws forth the subject of his inspiration from the fullness of a well-stored mind.

It is exceedingly difficult to follow the intricate arguments and speculations in which these alleged proofs of immortality are involved. Augustine, apparently, realised this when he wrote in his *Retractationes*: "Qui primo ratiocinationum contortione atque brevitate sic obscurus

[1] *Ennead* IV, book vii, 15.

est, ut fatiget, cum legitur, etiam intentionem meam vixque intelligatur a me ipso."[1] He confesses, it is seen, some forty years after they had been proposed, that these metaphysical proofs are not only vague and confused, but even unintelligible.

This purely speculative method of reasoning for the presentation and development of what may be termed the natural evidences of immortality was abandoned by Augustine in later years. By far the best and most acceptable of all the arguments proposed by him to prove the immortality of the human soul is based upon man's natural desire to prolong his existence. "Every man," Augustine writes, "is aware of a deep-seated, ineradicable, natural longing for being and for life. This desire is one of those fundamental cravings which belong to our common, rational, human nature. We all have a desire to live. No one wishes to be annihilated.[2] Our nature shrinks from the very thought of annihilation.[3] So powerful is this longing for existence that were a man who is actually miserable to be given the alternative of continuing in a state of misery or of being annihilated, he would unhesitatingly choose the former. This instinct of self-preservation is seen also in brute creation. Trees and plants, also, after their own fashion, manifest something similar to this tendency, as can be seen from the way in which their roots extend down deep into the soil while their branches stretch skywards towards the sun in order that they may draw from these sources what is necessary for the continuance of life.[4] In the latter case, it is true,

[1] i. 5.
[2] De Trin., xiii, 3.
[3] De Civ. Dei, xi, 27.
[4] De Civ. Dei, xi, 27.

this tendency does not imply conscious effort. The irrational animal, on the other hand, strives consciously in the struggle for existence. In the human being, however, there is present both conscious effort and the rational desire to survive. Man desires not merely to survive his present existence, but he actually desires to be immortal.[1] This desire has been implanted in man by the supremely immutable Creator; therefore, it will never be frustrated, and man will continue to exist for ever.

Another argument for the immortality of the soul given by Augustine is that of man's natural desire for happiness. He speaks of this universal desire "omnium certa sententia est, qui ratione quoquo modo uti possunt, beatos esse omnes homines velle."[2] In addition to recognising in himself this longing for happiness, each man knows that this desire is not proper to himself as an individual, but that it is shared also by every other human being.[3] All men may not be aware of this universal desire, nor of the best means of securing this happiness. Augustine, however, agrees with the Platonists that this desire for happiness can only be fully realised by the possession of the Supreme Good.[4] The Supreme Good, Augustine says, is God, and He is unattainable in this mortal state; therefore, if man is to be happy, he must survive his present existence. Unless, however, this survival is permanent, man could not really be happy, since he would always live in fear of losing that which he possessed and enjoyed.[5] Man, therefore, cannot be really

[1] *De Trin.*, xiii, 8.
[2] *De Civ. Dei*, x, 1.
[3] *De Trin.*, xiii, 3.
[4] *De Civ. Dei*, x, 1.
[5] *Ibid.*

happy without immortality. "Cum ergo beati esse omnes homines velint, si vere volunt, profecto et esse immortales volunt; aliter enim beati esse non possent." This twofold desire for happiness and immortality has been implanted in the nature of man by the Creator; therefore, it will not be frustrated.[1]

Augustine argues about the inability of even the best intellects to solve the problem of immortality.[2] He quotes the opinion of Plato, Plotinus, and Porphyry, and the unsatisfactory conclusions at which they arrived. He, therefore, states that the whole question of immortality rests ultimately on faith. "It is faith that promises not by human argumentation, but by divine authority, that the whole man, that is, soul and body, will be immortal and therefore truly blessed."[3] This is one of the reasons why the Son of Man assumed our mortal nature; it is in order that we may one day partake of that immortality which He alone can give.[4]

Augustine's doctrine of immortality has a certain degree of merit. There are some writers who refer to this portion of his philosophy with merely a passing reference to the arguments in *De Immortalitate Animae*.[5] Other writers have failed to find anything of worth in his teaching on the immortality of the soul.[6] Nourrisson, on the other hand, treats of the proofs given by Augustine in his earlier years[7]. No student, however, who is anxious to understand the teaching of this great writer, can

[1] *De Trin.*, xiii, 8.
[2] *De Trin.*, xiii, 9.
[3] *Ibid.*
[4] *Ibid.*
[5] Ueberweg-Heinze, ii, p. 134–135, Stoecke, Turner and others.
[6] *Cath. Ency*, ii, art. "Augustine," p. 84.
[7] *La Philosophie de Saint Augustin*. Paris. 1865.

disregard the principal arguments which are advanced in his two great works, *De Trinitate* and *De Civitate Dei*, written during the best years of his career. The argument based on man's natural craving for immortality as presented by St. Augustine is deserving of some serious consideration. It is an argument that has always made a strong, and sometimes a convincing, appeal to thoughtful men. It was probably through Augustine that this argument found its way into Scholastic philosophy, and, in the hands of Thomas Aquinas, it was developed into a strong rational support of the Christian doctrine of Immortality.

(vi) Summary of St. Augustine's Teaching on the subject of the Soul

It is possible to trace a resemblance between the Augustinian theories of psychology and those of recent times. The development of the latter is remarkable by reason of its employment in medical practice; the psychological study of the mind has been utilised, to a considerable degree, to discover the causes of functional nervous disorders in the unconscious. Consequently, terms such as "balance," "equilibrium," "harmony," and "complex," have come into general use. In the terminology of Augustine the words "harmony," "proportion," "order," and "unity," are often mentioned; he especially emphasises the meaning of the words "desire" and "satisfaction." This peculiarity was premeditated. "Nulla est causa philosophandi nisi ut beati simus." His ideas on the subject of being and love are explained by means of the Pythagorean and Platonic theories of numbers.

The teaching of modern psychology on the subject of the necessity of healthy functioning impulses and dynamic dispositions is in agreement with that of St. Augustine. In both systems of teaching there is the same emphasis laid on the term "desire." Modern investigation, indeed, explained the working of various complexes and the interrelation of conation, cognition, and emotion of which Augustine was ignorant, yet, it must be admitted that his teaching corrects and supplements the conclusions of modern psychology. He assumes as fundamental the longing of our nature, and thereby anticipates the "Libido" which plays so prominent a part in Jung's Psychology. He believes that character is rightly developed by integration, and that when it is so developed, the health of the individual is thereby safeguarded.

He emphasises the need of the mind for a well-defined goal of effort, and in this may be said to anticipate Adler's teaching on the necessity for a "life-purpose." In claiming that we possess a unique faculty which works indefatigably towards the attainment of this goal, correcting volitional aberrations and gradually effecting singleness of aim and consequent unification of the mind, Augustine, as we now know, was misconceiving an important truth. There is no unique faculty which controls the mind. The falsity of the faculty psychology, however, has only been exposed quite recently. Nevertheless, it remains true that co-ordination of purposes leads to integration of "personality."

The character of the personality thus developed depends upon the nature of the end towards which the mind is striving. There are, of course, proximate ends of action; but behind these there may be, and ought to be, a remote end which qualifies nearer ends and influences the choice alternating between. Modern psychology, as Trotter has so effectively demonstrated in his book on

"The Instincts of the Herd in Peace and War," is unable to supply any more satisfactory goal than a working adjustment between the mind and the world as it is at present. St. Augustine makes good this defect by taking, as it were, the cover off the casket of the soul and revealing, neither the "libido" of Jung, nor the "wish-fulfilment" of Freud, nor the "individual self-assertion" of Adler, but a love for transcendent beauty and overwhelming goodness. Whereas modern psychology provides only corrections for the conflicts and maladjustments in the subconscious mind, here is an end which affords satisfaction to the highest cravings of our own conscious being.

St. Augustine formulated the Christian concept of the human soul and contributed largely to its development. He collected and condensed the principal ideas and arguments on the subject which he discovered in Pagan philosophy, interpreting and explaining these in the light of Christian teaching. Although he was a profound philosopher and an intelligent psychologist, his chief interest in all problems relating to the human soul was, as we have said elsewhere, not of a philosophical or a psychological character, but rather theological.

His most remarkable contribution to the Christian philosophy of the human soul is his development of the doctrine of its spiritual nature. He was probably the first Christian thinker to understand clearly the distinction between matter and spirit, body and substance. He stands out among the philosophers of his time as the uncompromising upholder of the doctrine that the soul of man is not a body, but a simple spiritual substance. The arguments, which he advanced to prove the correctness of his teaching, constitute a permanent bulwark of defence against the ever-recurring attacks of materialism. His appeal to the authority of consciousness in his proof of this doctrine, and his insistence on the scientific value of the data obtainable by introspection, have ensured for him an exalted position among those who have aided in the development of psychological method. The philosophical doctrine of spirituality outlined by him is as important as any which has been attempted since his day; it is not an exaggeration to say, that, so far as this aspect of Christian philosophy is concerned, he was the richest contributor in the long history of Christian thought.

As regards the doctrine of immortality, he was evidently influenced by the teaching of Plato, when, at the commencement of his life as a Christian, he formulated the metaphysical proof of the soul's immortality. The development of the argument based on the universal desire for immortality, however, was peculiarly his own, and is a distinct contribution to the teaching on the subject.

His prolonged investigation of the origin of the human soul resulted in his arriving at a clearer and better understanding of the nature of the soul. Although he never pronounced definitely in favour of any particular theory of the origin of the soul, he appears to prefer Generationism as the theory best suited to his defence of the orthodox doctrine of original sin against the Pelagians. It is well known that this theory has long since been set aside by Christian philosophical and theological circles in favour of the special Creation theory advanced by Jerome, and several centuries later by Thomas Aquinas.

A knowledge of St. Augustine's teaching on the subject of the human soul is helpful to enable us to understand the development of psychological thought from his day to the end of the thirteenth century. Every

Christian thinker of any note, who appeared during this period, was more or less under the influence of this great Patristic philosopher. Albertus Magnus and Thomas Aquinas were undoubtedly more directly and powerfully dominated by the philosophy of Aristotle, but they were also influenced to a considerable degree by St. Augustine. Thomas Aquinas not only appeals frequently to the authority of Augustine, but also repeats many of the arguments which had been formulated by him. In the hands of this Master-Scholastic of the thirteenth century, the Christian concept of the human soul was perfected and woven into that "perennial philosophy which has been the rich heritage of subsequent centuries."[1]

[1] O'Connor. *Concept of the Human Soul*, p. 77.

Chapter VI

FREEDOM OF THE WILL

One of the most remarkable consequences of basing philosophy upon an anthropological foundation is, in Augustine's teaching, the important functions which he assigned, in his theory of the Universe, to the will. The chief motive, doubtless, which influenced him to adopt this view was the result of his own experience. His nature was ardent and his will was strong. As he analysed his own feelings, he recognised his will as his most important faculty. Consequently, he believed the will to be the most important faculty in all men. "Omnes nihil aliud quam voluntates sunt."

The psychology of St. Augustine is, certainly, very different from that of other writers. He emphasises the importance of the will in a very striking manner. He refers to the controlling influence of the will in the process of ideation and the acquisition of knowledge.[1] The Neo-Platonists distinguished between the state of sense stimulation and of becoming conscious of the same. Augustine, on the other hand, demonstrates, by careful analysis of the act of seeing, that becoming conscious is essentially the result of will (intentio animi.) As concentration is, accordingly, a matter of the will, so the operation of the inner sense (sensus interior) reveals an analogous dependence upon the will. To bring our mental states and bodily actions into consciousness depends upon our concentration.

The climax of Augustine's teaching on the subject of the freedom of the will appears, when he asserts that the

[1] *Cf. De Trin.*, xi.

consciousness of the intellect (ratiocinatio), and the mental operations of judging and reasoning, depend on the action of the will. The will determines the result of both sensations and feelings.

In the more important parts of the teaching of St. Augustine the chief factor is his conception of the freedom of the will. Because the will is free, a decision, a choice, or an assent of the will may be regarded as independent of the functions of the understanding. Augustine defends his position against various objections. He teaches the doctrine of man's consciousness of ethical and religious responsibility. He wishes to uphold the claims of divine justice.

The Alexandrians, indeed, held the theory of Indifferentism. The will, according to their view, always decides in favour of the stronger motive, whatever that motive may be. When, however, the soul, through union with Christ, is sufficiently purified from sin, then the stronger motive in the soul is always good. But man's will, at all stages of his development, is the slave of his own desire. Thus, man is free, because his action follows from his own desire. Adam desired to sin and, therefore, fell from a state of innocence. And all men since have been prone to desire evil rather than good. Nevertheless, man is still free to desire amendment, and when he so desires, the will chooses and decides accordingly. This, presumably, is virtue rather than salvation. Salvation comes through the changed desire which follows from the union of the soul with Christ.[1]

In Augustine's teaching on the subject of the freedom of the will the exigencies of philosophical and theological controversy led him to make contradictory statements.

[1] Bigg. *The Christian Platonists of Alexandria*, p. 334.

He advocated freedom of the will in opposition to Manichaeism fatalism. In thus emphasising the freedom of the will and the impossibility of sin apart from the will of the sinner, Augustine appears to have gone too far. Consequently, in his controversy with Pelagius and Caelestius, who laid such emphasis upon the power of the will, he was compelled to qualify and restate his teaching about freedom, in order to defend his doctrine of Grace. In so doing, he approximated to that theory of fatalism which he so earnestly opposed in the system of the Manichaeans.

As an illustration of the fact that Augustine changed the formulation of his teaching on this subject we may refer to his treatise against the Manichaeans, in which he argued that sin existed nowhere but in the will, otherwise the sinner could not be accounted guilty[1] ("Quibus concessis colligerem nusquam scilicet nisi in voluntate esse peccatum; cum mihi auxiliaretur etiam illud quod justitia peccantes tenet sola mala voluntate, quamvis quod voluerint implere nequiverint"). This teaching repudiates the Alexandrian view that the will is the mere instrument of the stronger motive or desire.

In opposition to this teaching on the subject of the will, the Pelagians maintained that this theory implied that infants are guilty of original sin before they have made any evil choice. He felt compelled, therefore, to explain[2] his teaching and to attribute the whole problem to the will of Adam. Thus he made it difficult for the Pelagians to emphasise unduly the will of the individual.

It is interesting to study Augustine's explanation of the

[1] *De duab. anim. cont. Manich.*, x, 12.
[2] *Retractations*, xv, 2.

will of Adam. He asserts that the soul of the first man, before he sinned, controlled his body with perfect freedom of will.[1] He not only had free will, but this was influenced in the direction of God.[2] If Adam had no freewill, he would have been unable to sin, but he would not have been a rational creature. In consequence of the Fall, man lost that complete freedom which he once enjoyed. The step in the argument which is here passed over was, no doubt, hidden from Augustine and from many succeeding generations of theologians. Modern thought, however, is acutely aware of this missing step. "In consequence of the Fall, Adam lost. . . . (But, Adam, through heredity, handed down to subsequent generations a tainted soul.) Therefore, mankind lost. . . ." This assumes Traducianism and excludes Creationism.

Augustine points out that there were certain limitations to the perfect freedom of Adam before the Fall. Though created free, Adam was ignorant of his future sin. If he had chosen to continue in this happy state and had not sinned, he would never have known death or misery.[3] The difference between Adam and the unfallen angels appears to be that the latter had no possibility of falling, whereas it was possible for Adam to have remained in a state of perfection or to have fallen. His will could have enabled him to avoid falling into sin. ("Quod adjutorium si homo ille (Adam) per liberum non deseruisset arbitrium, semper esset bonus.")[4] In other words, Adam's liberty consisted in being able to avoid sinning ("posse non peccare"), whereas the liberty of the unfallen angels

[1] Ep., 143.
[2] De Civ. Dei, xiv, 12–15.
[3] De Cor. et Grat., xxviii.
[4] De Cor. et Grat., xxxi.

consisted in being incapable of sinning ("non posse peccare").[1] That is to say they were certain of choosing only what is good.

The fall of Adam necessitated the "gratia Dei," to enable him to do good. We are, accordingly, prepared for the assertion that original sin must be traced to its source which is freedom. The will, therefore, was the originator of evil.[2] All the tendencies to evil, with which we were born, owe their origin to Adam's freedom.[3] Although Adam was endowed with the power of avoiding evil, yet he was not willing to abide in his state of perfection.[4] Augustine frequently asserts his doctrine of the freedom of the will when referring to original sin. "Man was lost by free will."[5] The evil which man contracts at birth proceeds from the will ("sed ex humana voluntate venientem in originis labe contraxit.")[6]

In reference to his statement that the misuse of man's free will was the cause of Adam's fall and that thereby the will of the whole race was infected, the question may be asked: "Does Augustine still maintain the freedom of will of each person?" An examination of his writings proves that he emphasises the belief that all evil is to be traced to a free choice of the will.[7] Sin exists by virtue of free will, since man sins if he wills it. ("Fit enim ut sit peccatum per liberum arbitrium, cum homo peccat, si velit.")[8]

[1] De Cor. et Grat., xxxii.
[2] De Civ. Dei, xiii, 15.
[3] Op. Imp. c. Jul., vi, 5.
[4] De Cor. et Grat., xxxii.
[5] Serm., clxxiv, 2.
[6] De Pec. Orig., xlvi; cf. also De Nupt. et Concup., i, 26.
[7] De Lib. Arbit., iii 2; iii 29; Retract., i, 9, etc.
[8] Op. Imp. c. Jul., iv, 101.

No sin can be committed without free will.[1] Even the controverted passage of Romans, vii, 19 ("non enim quod volo, hoc ago; sed quod nolo, hoc facio") must not be interpreted in such a manner as to negative free will.[2] In one passage[3] in which sin and original sin are clearly distinguished, Augustine affirms that both proceed from the will.

Augustine even denies the necessity of sin.[4] God has never compelled man to sin ("non cogente Deo"),[5] but he has sinned simply because he willed it. This aspect of his doctrine is chiefly emphasised in order to oppose the teaching of Manichaeism. He is not willing to admit that fatalism can in any way nullify man's freedom.

It is difficult, however, to reconcile St. Augustine's teaching on the subject of God's foreknowledge, as expounded in De Civ. Dei, v, with his doctrine of the freedom of the will. Augustine asserts that God foreknew that man would sin and thus bring death upon himself, and, also, that children doomed to mortality would be born.[6] Nevertheless, he maintains that it is man himself who sins. Whether man wills to sin or not, God foreknows it.[7]

The difficulty is somewhat nullified by his teaching that the "Gratia Dei" is needed to enable fallen man to do good, and that God foreknew upon whom He would bestow this gift. ("Omnia porro dona sua, et quibus ea

[1] De Pec. Mer. et Rem., i, 65.
[2] Retract. I, xiii, 5; xv, 3.
[3] De Nupt. et Concup. ii, 48.
[4] Cont. Faust., xxii, 22.
[5] Op. Imp. c. Jul., V, lxiii.
[6] Cf. Civ. Dei, v, 9–10; De Cor. et Grat., xxvii.
[7] De Civ. Dei, v, 10.

fuerat largiturus, deum praescisse negare non possunt.")[1]
By this explanation Augustine tries to justify himself
while adhering to his teaching on man's freedom and
God's prescience.[2] ("Quocirca nullo modo cogimur,
aut retenta praescientia Dei tollere voluntatis arbitrium
aut retento voluntatio arbitrio Deum (quod nefas est)
negare praescium futurorum sed utrumque amplectimur.")
It is somewhat difficult to reconcile the doctrine of the
freedom of the will with the teaching of Augustine that
our free choice is foreknown by God.

It appears that there was a very cogent reason why
Augustine could not relinquish the postulate of divine
foreknowledge. The atonement, by means of the
crucifixion, was the eternal purpose of God. And this
implies knowledge that man would sin and thus need
redemption.

The dilemma is escaped when it is recognised that
God's purpose was to reveal Himself, and that, apart
from man's sin, the revelation would have been given.
The effect of sin was not to necessitate the Incarnation,
but to delay it, and further, to bring to pass the crucifixion as the consequence of the revelation of God in
Jesus Christ. The abuse of his freedom by man was not
the necessary condition of the Incarnation. Atonement
is union with God, which can be effected by revelation
without redemption. Because of sin, atonement has to
include redemption from evil.

As the result of the Pelagian controversy, this ardent
advocate of freedom is by degrees transformed, perhaps
unconsciously, into a determinist. Pelagius did not feel
the need of external aid, the "gratia Dei," as Augustine

[1] *De Don. Persev.*, lxvi.
[2] *Cf. De Civ. Dei*, v, 9.

did, for the former had not yielded to self-indulgence as the latter had in his earlier years. Pelagius believed that to speak of grace was only another way of expressing his belief in free will, and that God's assistance consisted chiefly in man's right use of free-will'[1] He argued that man can avoid sin by free will alone,[2] and that all men may be sinless if they choose.[3] It was Caelestius, the disciple of Pelagius, who developed the arguments on this teaching to their logical conclusion; he taught, also, that Adam's sin injured only himself, and not the race, and that new-born infants are as perfect as Adam before his fall. Augustine, consequently, was impelled to challenge such a misinterpretation of his teaching on the subject of freedom.

Pelagius had taken offence, indeed, before the outbreak of the great controversy, at Augustine's famous sentence: "Grant what thou commandest, and command what thou dost desire."

Pelagianism was the natural outcome of the teaching of Christian rationalism which had for a long time been diffused throughout the West, especially among the more cultured, who had been educated in the popular philosophy which was influenced by Stoicism and Aristotelianism and had, as the result of the influence of Julian, a tendency towards naturalism. Nature, freewill, virtue, and law—strictly defined and made independent of the notion of God—were the catchwords of Pelagianism. Self-taught virtue is the supreme good which is followed by reward. Religion and morality are the result of the operation of the free spirit of man, and can, accordingly,

---

[1] *De Grat. et Lib. Arbit.*, xxiii, 26; *De Spir. et Lit.*, iv; *De Grat. Christi*, iii.
[2] *De Grat. Christi*, xxix.
[3] *De Nupt. et Concup.*, ii.

become the ornament of the individual at any moment by man's own effort.

When attacking the doctrine of Pelagius, Augustine formulates his teaching upon the subject in a somewhat perplexing manner, and he even speaks of a necessity of sinning in every person since Adam. He speaks of a necessary tendency to sin (quaedam peccandi necessitas),[1] which is the result of those tendencies which have vitiated our nature. He qualified this statement, however, by adding that these tendencies may be removed by the operation of grace, and thus complete liberty may be enjoyed.[2] This teaching appears to mean that there is a necessity of sinning, which is the punishment of sin committed without necessity. ("Multum erras, qui vel necessitatem nullam putas esse peccandi, vel cum non intelligis illius peccati esse poenam, quod nulla necessitate commisum est.")[3] Augustine had no intention of denying freedom. His great object is to refute the belief that by mere strength of will man can live a righteous life. He earnestly desired that the "gratia Dei" should be fully recognised.

A distinction drawn between sins and sinfulness, i.e. between the committing of sins and the sinfulness of the soul when alienated from God, would have helped Augustine at this point. It is the sinfulness of the soul which is "of necessity," not the performance of specific sinful acts.

The dependence of the human will on divine co-operation serves as the basis of a very earnest appeal for strength. "Order, I pray, and command whatever Thou

[1] *De Nat. et Grat.*, lxxix.
[2] *De Nat. et Grat.*, lxxix.
[3] *Op. Imp. c. Jul.* I, cv; *De Nat. et Grat.*, lxxx.

dost wish, but heal me and open mine eyes, that I may see Thy guiding. Drive folly far from me, that I may discover Thee."[1] In these words we recognise a profound consciousness of inability, apart from divine enlightenment and support. The writer of the *Soliloquies* regards God as the source of strength.

We are still in a state of uncertainty, however, for if every man since the time of Adam lives under this "quaedam necessitas" and can only be liberated by an outside power, can his condition properly be described as free? If man performs no good deed, which God does not cause him to do,[2] in what way does man enjoy freedom?

In his endeavour to conjoin the two ideas of freedom and the need of God's grace, Augustine refers to the eye as an illustration. When it is enveloped in darkness and no attempt is made to use it for its natural purpose, the eye is self-sufficient. But, to be of use, the eye needs the aid of external light.[3] He insists on the necessity of co-operating grace and free-will as the secret of a happy and successful life.[4]

In order to understand clearly what Augustine's teaching about the freedom of the will really is, it is important to recognise that he uses the term *"freedom"* with at least *four distinct meanings;* otherwise we shall charge him with self-contradiction.

(1) He frequently employs the term in a *general* sense as the power which distinguishes man from a machine. The term means simple spontaneity or self-activity, as

---

[1] *Solil.*, i, 3.

[2] *Cont. duas Ep. Pelag.* ii, 21.

[3] *De Gest. Pelag.*, 7.

[4] *Op. Imp. c. Jul.*, VI, xxvi; *De Pec. Mer. et Remis.*, ii, 6; *De Spir. et Lit.*, xv.

opposed to action under external constraint, or as the result of animal instinct. Both sin and holiness are voluntary, that is to say, acts of the will and not the result of natural necessity. It is a man's power to choose between two alternative courses of action. He writes: "voluntas est animi motus, cogente nullo, ad aliquid vel non ammittendum, vel adipiscendum."[1] It is enjoyed by angels and demons as well as by man; it is the distinguishing mark between man and the animals. This freedom belongs at all times to the human will, even in the sinful state (in which the will is, strictly speaking, self-willed).

(2) A freedom that was enjoyed by Adam alone, which Augustine defines as "posse non peccare." It was in the power of Adam to will what was right or to will what was wrong ("sic enim oportebat prius hominem fieri, ut et bene velle posset, et male.")[2] This is the most natural meaning of the term "freedom."

(3) The limited freedom enjoyed by man since the fall of Adam implies a freedom to sin ("nam neque liberum arbitrium quidquam nisi ad peccandum valet.")[3] The term "posse non peccare" no longer is true. Man is no longer able to resist sin. His freedom consists in the ability to sin.[4] Without God's help his choice is only evil.[5] It is not a choice between sin and holiness, but between actions within the sphere of sinfulness and of "justitia civilis."[6] Augustine does not appear to appreciate the

[1] *De Duab. Anim.*, xiv.
[2] *Enchir.*, cv; also *De Cor. et Grat.*, xxxii.
[3] *De Spir. et Lit.*, v.
[4] *Enchir.*, xxx.
[5] *Serm.*, 156, 11.
[6] *Cont. Duas Epis. Pelag.* ii, 5.

difficulty, why the will which is free to choose sin is not also free to choose righteousness. His only explanation is that sin and lust arise from the act of the will, whereas the impulse to good does not arise within, but comes to us from God.[1]

(4) There remains a fourth meaning of the term "freedom" which is frequently used by Augustine. It has reference to the highest degree of freedom, the free decision of self-determination of the will towards the good and holy. It is to be exercised in the next life by the righteous. Adam, before the Fall, had the power to do good or evil, but in the future world there will only be the freedom to do good. ("Postea vero sic erit ut male vella non possit.")[2] It is a "felix necessitas boni," and cannot, because it will not, sin.

Augustine insists that this condition is one of real freedom. Man himself drives out the tendency to sin from his mind. The "posse non peccare" may be described as *formal* freedom, the "non posse peccare" may be termed *real* freedom. It must be mentioned, however, that the former species of freedom is enjoyed only by Adam, and the latter by the saint. It is the highest stage of moral development. To serve God is true freedom.[3] According to Augustine, man's only possibility of doing good depends on the aid of the "gratia Dei."

Augustine, in his work, *De Libero Arbitrio*, also discusses the problem of the will. This treatise forms part of his explanation of his deliverance from Dualism; it was, undoubtedly, intended to facilitate the return to Catholicism of several companions, whom he had previously

[1] *De Pat.*, xiii, 14.
[2] *Enchir.*, cv; *Op. Imp. c. Jul.*, VI, xii.
[3] *De Civ. Dei*, xiv, 11.

influenced to adopt the Manichaean religion. The third book of this treatise was written at Hippo several years after the writing of Books i and ii, and its contents display a theological development far in advance of the writings which belong to an earlier time.

The problem discussed in this work is whether God is the author of evil. The first part consists of an analysis of *what evil is*. Evil may be said to be of two kinds, moral and physical, that is to say, what we do and what we suffer. As to the former, if goodness is an essential attribute of God, moral evil cannot possibly be derived from Him. As to the latter, if righteousness is one of His attributes, He will not only reward the good, but also punish the wicked. Physical evil, therefore, proceeds from God. Of moral evil, however, he says that there is no one author to whom its existence can be ascribed. Every individual is the author of his own evil doings.

In one of his other works[1] Augustine asserts that the cause of evil is to be found in the will, which turns aside from what is the higher to what is lower, e.g. the pride of those angels and men, who turned away from God, Who has absolute being, to think only of themselves, whose being is limited. The inferior as such is not evil, but to incline to it from the higher state is evil. The evil will works that which is evil, but it is not moved by any positive cause; it has no "causa efficiens"; but only a "causa deficiens."

Evil is not a substance or a nature (essence) but a marring of nature (the essence) of what is good. It is a "defect," a "privation," or "loss of good," diminution of integrity, of beauty, of happiness, of virtue; where there

[1] *De Civ. Dei*, xii, 6 *seq.*

is no violation of good, there is no evil: "esse vitium et non nocere non potest."

Evil, therefore, can only exist as an adjunct of what is good, and that, not of the immutably, but only of the mutably good. An absolute good is possible, but absolute evil is impossible.[1]

Augustine tells us that the problem of the origin of evil perplexed him greatly as a young man and led him astray into non-Christian systems of thought, and involved him in many difficulties, from which he would never have escaped if he had not received divine help in answer to his earnest prayer for truth. Augustine then explains the way by which he escaped the difficulties entailed by the doctrine of necessity. The problem is as follows: If sin originates from the soul, and the soul from God, the conclusion appears to be that sin originates from God.

Augustine emphasises the importance of arriving at a right conception of God when considering the problem, "Optime namque de Deo existimare verissimum est pietatis exordium." He writes: "No man can enjoy the highest conception of God without recognising Him to be the unchanging Creator of all good which He transcends." We ask, therefore, what is the essential nature of evil?

It is not sufficient to answer that what constitutes evil is the fact of prohibition by human law. Human law has, at times, forbidden what was absolutely right, such as a belief in Christ. Law varies with place and time, according to the exigencies of civil life.

Superior to all human law, which is only of a temporary character, there is eternal law. From this all

[1] De Civ. Dei, xi, 22; xii, 3.

temporal law derives its sanction. This eternal law is deeply implanted in the human mind and heart and ought never to be transgressed. The harmony of the life of the individual is secured by obeying the precepts of the eternal law. When men subject the mind to the domination of impulse and inclination and then listen to the promptings of the will, misery is the natural result. On the other hand, if the will obeys the precepts of the eternal law, and regards obedience to the law in preference to temporal things, the consequence is goodness with its resultant happiness.

Augustine says that no man can enjoy happiness simply by seeking it. Happiness can be attained only by the will to live aright. Happiness, accordingly, depends upon the will. Evil, on the other hand, arises from misdirected freedom.

The question arises: "Why was freedom allowed?" In his controversy with Euodius, Augustine declares that, whereas free-will is a gift from God and is permitted to operate for the purpose of doing right, yet, because some men divert it with the intention of doing wrong, we ought not to challenge God as to the character of His gift.

He then proceeds to answer the question whether free-will is to be regarded as one of those things that are good. He maintains that man cannot live aright without free-will, therefore it must be good. Evil is the result of concentrating the will away from the things of God. This turning away from God is voluntary.

Augustine endeavours to distinguish[1] the will to act from the act of the will. An act of the will is concentrated not only on the present, but, also, when we think of

[1] *De Immort. Anim.*, iii, 3.

the termination of the act, on the future. There are, accordingly, two aspects of every act—the timeless and the time aspect, into which the former is changed.

He also asserts that, without will, no knowledge is possible; and, on the other hand, without knowledge we cannot exercise will. Will, accordingly, is the forerunner of knowledge and leads also to action. The possibility of knowledge without an act or will is not implied in the doctrine of *Assent*. In *Cont. Acad.* ii, 9, Augustine attacked the teaching of the Academy which had removed the word "Assent" from its vocabulary. The function of the will in acquiring knowledge is involved in the doctrine that Ratio precedes Scientia. The latter is Visio, and the former is Aspectus. Aspectus is active, Visio is contemplative. We look in order to see but looking implies an act of will and thus by analogy knowledge results from the operation of will, for Ratio precedes Scientia. Ratio is active, implying an act of will; Scientia is the passive result.

The question of Assent is involved in the nature of *Deception*. It is possible to regard an object from a false standpoint without being deceived, if the person is unaware that the object is not in reality what it seems to him to be. We may conclude, therefore, that it is not the person who sees falsely who is deceived, but he who assents to false conditions. (Confitendum est igitur, non eum falli qui false videt, sed eum qui assentitur falsis.)[1]

The greater activity of the mind depends upon the activity of the will. Because it inhabits the body, the mind is continually subject to the influences of the body. It must be raised above these in order to exercise its true intellectual activity.

[1] *Solil.*, ii, 3, 3.

It is the will which liberates the mind from the trammels of sense and sets it working, and so, in the higher activities of the mind, such as thought, the mind divests itself consciously from the body. Who, after careful self-examination, has not discovered that, if he desires to think well, he must exalt his mind by abstraction, so to speak, above his bodily sensations?

Something more is conveyed by this statement than the mere demonstration of the abstract superiority of the mind over the body; it implies practical superiority through the operation of the will.[1]

The mind, thus regarded from the standpoint of Force (or will), is the strongest thing in the world. All which is not soul is body, and is inferior, and, therefore, weaker. God alone can rule the mind, for everyone will allow that He Who is superior to the rational soul is God.[2]

Augustine mentions elsewhere that, in order that "veritas" and the "scire deum et animam" may be able to become supreme, and, as it were, the unique function of man, the will must be called into operation on its behalf. This takes place through God's grace, which leads the soul to will and to love what is spiritual, i.e. God. In this way alone it becomes possible for the intellect to assume supremacy. Accordingly, to set free the will is, finally, the substitution of the supremacy of the intellect for that of the will, Yet, in so far as the supremacy of the intellect cannot maintain itself without the "amor essendi et sciendi," the will remains the co-efficient of the intellect, even in the highest sphere of man's operations.

[1] *De Immort. Anim.*, x.
[2] *De Immort. Anim.*, xiii.
[3] *Conf.*, ix, 24.

Such, briefly, is Augustine's view of the relation of the will to the intellect.

In *De Quant. Anim.*, xxxiii, Augustine treats of the different stages of the soul's development and the will is brought into prominence when he refers to Stage IV. In the previous stage, he treats of the genius of the human mind, but the operation of the will indicates a higher stage. The results of the operation of the intellect are noble, but if they appertain only to man, they are the heritage of all men, both bad and good. But, in the next higher stage is included goodness and praise which can be bestowed upon goodwill alone. We thus discover that Augustine has, almost verbally, anticipated Kant's dictum that the only unqualified good in the world is the goodwill.[1]

The soul, accordingly, can consciously become supreme over the operations of the body, when she believes that the world's goods are not comparable to her own goodness and beauty. The more the soul becomes pleased with herself, the more she withdraws from the vileness of the earth.

At the seventh stage, the will reposes in the complete attainment of its highest desires, in the vision of, and in the contemplation of, the Truth itself. It is the place of highest bliss.

Augustine's last treatises, *De Predestinatione Sanctorum*, and *De Dono Perseverantiae*, are intended to controvert the semi-Pelagian doctrine, as held especially by Cassianus, who admitted that man can accomplish nothing good without grace, but ascribed the beginning of every good work, which God's grace alone can bring to completion, to the free will of man himself. He could not

[1] *De Quant. Anim.*, xxxiii, 73.

admit that God would save only a portion of the human race and that Christ died only for the elect. Augustine, on the contrary, teaches the doctrine of all-determining, antecedent grace, and that even the commencement of good in man is dependent on such grace. Jerome, however, in the *Dialogus Contra Pelagianos* (composed about A.D. 415) maintains that man can determine himself in favour of good or evil, but only with the assistance of grace he can accomplish the good.

The Augustinian explanation of the Divine government of wills is original, profound, and but little known. Augustine ascribes the value of a moral act to the inward disposition and the divine direction of the will; he judges of this from the standpoint of the whole life and according to the standard of love to God, which is the soul of all true virtue.

The will never decides without a motive, without the attraction of some good which it perceives in the object. Although the will may be free in the contemplation of every motive, still, as a matter of fact, it forms different resolutions, according to the different motives presented to it.

Augustine observes that man is not the master of his first thoughts; he can exert an influence on the direction of his reflections, but he cannot determine the objects, the images, and, consequently, the motives, which present themselves to his mind. As chance is only a word, it is God who determines, according to His pleasure, these first perceptions of men, either by the providential action of exterior causes, or internally by a Divine illumination imparted to the soul.[1]

There are, indeed, intellectual difficulties in the system

[1] *Cath. Ency.*, vol. I, p. 96.

of Augustine which reveal many inconsistencies. Augustine is compelled to admit that men still retain their freedom, in spite of the Fall, and yet he declares that they can do no good. This is not true freedom, whatever else it may be. He admits that sin results from the will, yet it is inherited sin that dominates his doctrinal system; men will be lost as the result of inherited sin, even when no wilful sin has been committed. In shifting the problem of the origin of sin from man's present condition to the initial transgression of Adam, so far from drawing nearer to a solution, his teaching simply intensifies the difficulty; for sin in man, as he now is, is explicable on account of his possessing a sinful nature, but it is inexplicable as the result of Adam's sin, who, "ex hypothesi," was created good.

Augustine seems to have been severely handicapped in his thought by the conception of the will as a "faculty." But a will which is not willing some choice is non-existent. It is not true, psychologically, to speak of man as possessing a will, or having will-power, or exercising his will. What we mean by will is the whole mind making a choice. In the same way, conscience is the whole mind making a moral decision. But it is the mind as a whole, and not a part of the mind called "the will," which is active.

Thus the problem of grace and free-will is eased. Grace is not a power which replaces or reinforces, or overrides "the will." Grace is the divine influence to which the mind as a unity responds. Grace is the personal influence of God upon our souls, and under this influence our souls attain to their highest potentiality. The good will is just the activity of the consecrated soul. Grace is the enrichment of the whole personality.

CHAPTER VII

THE EPISTEMOLOGY OF ST. AUGUSTINE

Summary of Chapter

The Importance of Epistemology—The Soul and Human Faculties—Knowledge through the Senses—Nature of Sense Perception—External Sense (a) Vision; (b) Nature of Sound; (c) Sense of Smell—Impressions to the Inner Man—Self-examination—Memory and Understanding—Instincts — Intellectual Desires — Admiration — Physico-Psychology: Weeping — Crowd Psychology — Child Psychology — Internal Sense — Observation—Interior Illumination—Affective-tone: (a) Pain; (b) Pleasure — Conation: Desire and Will — Certitude — Perception and Cognition — Memory — Imagination — Phantasia — Hallucination, etc. — Psychic-Physical Phenomena — The Subconscious and Memory — The Sub-Conscious — Dreams — Rational Faculties — Ratio and Ratiocinatio—The Disciplinae.

The Importance of Epistemology

Epistemology is that branch of philosophy which is concerned with the value of human knowledge. It does not merely treat of certain assumptions of science, but also undertakes to test the cognitive faculty itself in all its functions.

It may be said that the Fathers of the Church were engaged chiefly in defending Christian dogmas, and thus, indirectly, in proving the harmony of revealed truth with reason. Augustine, however, goes farther than any other early writer in the analysis of knowledge and in the inquiry concerning its validity. In his treatise *Contra Academicos*, he opposes the teaching of the sceptics of the Academy, who recognised no certain, but only probable, knowledge. What is probability, he asks in an argument "ad hominem," but a likeness of, or an approach to, truth and certitude? Accordingly, how can any one speak of probability who does not first recognise the principles of certitude? He asserts that the fact of doubting and the possibility of being deceived imply existence.

The study of Epistemology which was undertaken by Augustine was continued by Descartes[1] and at a later time by Locke, who tells us that his purpose was to discover "the certainty, evidence and extent " of human knowledge.[2] Hume subsequently challenged the security of Locke's whole system.[3]

During recent years Epistemology has come to the front in the study of philosophical sciences. In the beginning of philosophical investigation, knowledge and certitude were accepted as self-evident facts which did not require discussion; but such questions as, "Is the attainment of certain knowledge within man's power?" "How does Knowledge arise?" have come up for consideration in recent times.

The importance of Epistemology cannot be overestimated, as it treats of the basis of knowledge itself, and, therefore, of all scientific, philosophical, oral, and religious principles.

The Soul and Human Faculties

The word "Spirit" is, certainly, a Biblical term for the highest aspect of man's life. It is a conception inseparable from the idea of man's relation to God, whether in creation or redemption. Throughout the Old Testament it is the most expressive term for human life: "The spirit (rûah) returns to God Who gave it."[4] In this way the psychology of the Bible must be distinguished from

---

[1] *Discours de la Méthode.*
[2] Locke. *Essay concerning Human Understanding,* I, 1, 3.
[3] *A Treatise of Human Nature.*
[4] Eccl., xii, 7.

that of all ethnic systems. The term "spirit" is not so used by Plato, by Philo, by the earlier Stoics, by Plotinus, the Neo-Platonists, nor indeed anywhere except in Biblical teaching. It suggests the direct dependence of man upon God.

This peculiarly Biblical idea indicates what is the highest in man, that which is common to God and man. "Spirit" (πνεῦμα) is the God-given principle of man's life—physical, mental and spiritual. Soul (ψυχή) is the Subject or bearer of life and has as its Hebrew equivalent the word "nephesh." The character of the psychology of the Bible has been misinterpreted by those who distinguish Spirit, soul and heart as separate faculties, as they are different aspects of one indivisible inner life. All through Scripture πνεῦμα denotes life as coming from God, ψυχή denotes life as constituted in the man.

The Epistles of St. Paul and the other writings of the New Testament reveal that a new shade of meaning has been added to this term. That which is "spiritual" in man is influenced by the Spirit of God—the new spirit of regeneration. "Spirit" (πνεῦμα) is a term employed in reference to a renewed man.[1]

In the teaching of the Bible on the subject of anthropology, this doctrine of the "pneuma" in man is distinctive in character.

Although the word "heart" is used with considerable clearness and consistency throughout the Bible, to signify the inner, the most important, the hidden and ruling element in man's nature, yet the term, when translated into modern language, denotes as one of its meanings, "principles of action."

The chief use of the word "pneuma" is psychological,

[1] Rom., viii, 16.

inasmuch as it refers to the spiritual personality controlling different influences. The fuller meaning of the term is the result of Biblical and Christian teaching. Some writers, indeed, regard the term as one specially formulated by Christianity.

In St. Paul's use of the term we recognise a parallel or analogy between the spirit of man and the Divine Spirit. There is frequent and intimate association in the employment of the terms "Soul" and "Spirit," which occurs very often in the Bible; they are almost parallel psychological expressions. Each, however, implies at all times the characteristic distinction—"soul" indicates the individual and personal life, and "spirit" the principle of life.

There is another antithesis, more peculiarly Pauline, of the "spirit" and the "flesh." The Pauline use of these terms indicates a moral distinction, which belongs specially to Christian teaching. They occur chiefly in those passages where St. Paul is describing the conflict of the old nature, or the "old man" as he terms it, with the new nature of the "new man." Human nature manifests itself in the flesh and appears as contrasted with pneuma, the Divine nature, or the divinely originated and sustained new nature. Thus "flesh" appears finally, in distinct and presupposed antithesis to "pneuma," to signify the sinful state of human nature and in such a manner that this condition, described as "flesh," results in that sinful nature—"the flesh determined by sin."[1]

The "pneuma" in man, which is the element originally created by God, and which ought to rule or govern man's whole nature, is used by St. Paul to express the new nature divinely originated in the Christian; thus a direct antithesis is developed between "flesh" and "spirit," and

[1] Rom., viii, 3.

everything spiritual is a divine creation, according to that new nature.

St. Paul also contrasts the term "pneumatikon" with mind ("nous" or "sunesis"); this is an antithesis as it contrasts the action of the "understanding" in man with that of spiritual or ecstatic impulse in a Christian.[1]

It is easy to discover the influence which the teaching of St. Paul exercised upon the mind of St. Augustine.

According to the latter the spirit or soul of man is a substance different from the body,[2] at least relatively simple,[3] and therefore immortal.[4] It is so united with the body that it is everywhere present, although certain organs serve for the performance of certain functions, as the "cerebrum" for feeling, the "cerebellum" for voluntary motion.[5] But the spirit appears to be independent of the body, so that seven different conditions can be distinguished. The three lowest, "anima de corpore," "in corpore," "circa corpus," have been already distinguished by Aristotle, but there must be added "anima ad se," "in se," "ad Deum," "in Deo."[6] The true centre of the spiritual personality results from the will of man. Man is, strictly speaking, nothing else than will.[7]

Augustine differed from Plato in his teaching about the parts of the soul, although it is not easy to arrive at settled convictions as to the significance of Plato's exposition.

[1] I Cor., xiv, 14, 15.
[2] De Anim. et ejus Orig. ii, 2.
[3] De Trin., vi, 6, 8.
[4] Solil., De Immort. Anim.
[5] De Gen. ad Litt., vii, 13.
[6] De Immort. Anim.; De Quant. Anim.
[7] De Civ. Dei, xix, 6.

Grote[1] calls attention to discrepancies between the teaching of the "Phaedo" and that of the "Philebus," and questions whether the argument for immortality in the former treatise applies to all three parts of the soul, or only to the highest. He argues that Plato adapts his doctrines to suit the need in these various dialogues. Archer-Hind[2] prefers to attempt to reconcile these difficulties.

Plato in the *Republic*[3] divided the soul into λογισικόν and ἄλογον ἔιδος, the latter being subdivided into Emotional and Appetitive parts (θυμειδές and ἐπιθυμητικόν).

These divisions of the soul have specific parts of the body allotted to them. Some scholars, such as Archer-Hind, and Natorp, think that the three divisions which Plato mentions are not real parts, but different forms of activity. The soul in itself is eternal and uniform in its substance, but on entering into union with matter is compelled, more or less, to operate through matter and the terminology assigned to this combined action of soul and matter are θυμός; ἐπιθυμία and θυμειδές and ἐπιθυμητικόν are expressions which indicate the soul in certain material relations.

Whatever is the exact teaching of Plato on this subject, it is apparent that the doctrine of Augustine is very different. He teaches a "Faculty" psychology, but it is not to be supposed that by the term "Faculty" a "locally" separate part of the mind is meant.

Aristotle distinguishes between cognition (νοῦς) and conation (ὄρεξις) as ultimate mental functions. A new classification arose of cognition, feeling, and conation

---

[1] Grote. *Plato*, vol. II, p. 159. Murray, 1875.
[2] "Difficulties in the Platonic psychology," *Journal of Philology*, x. 1882.
[3] 434–441.

or will; feeling being used in the sense of affective consciousness.

Knowledge through the Senses

Human activity in the field of knowledge is treated of by Augustine under two heads—Sensus and Intellectus. ("Nam omne quod contemplamur, sive cogitatione capimus, aut sensu aut intellectu capimus.")[1] All we know is derived either from the senses or from the mind. The senses are called the "Interpreters" of the mind which it uses to acquire knowledge of the outer world.[2]

The senses are five in number[3] and a characteristic of sense knowledge is that these things which we know by its means are recognised as lying outside of us. This implies that no complete union between the object and the perceiving agent takes place and, therefore, this can lead to no true knowledge. This characteristic is further marked by the fact that the objects are restricted within space relations.[4]

The senses are no source of knowledge in the true and higher sense; they do not discover for us absolute or universal truth. They are the handmaids of the intellect; it is the mind which perceives rather than the senses. It is not the eyes themselves which see, nor the ears which hear, but the mind perceives by means of them.[5] The ears only catch up the sounds; comprehension of their meaning is the function of the mind.

Augustine often uses deprecatory language concerning

[1] De Immort. Anim., vi, 10.
[2] De Magist., xii, 39.
[3] De Lib. Arbit., ii, 3, 8.
[4] De Immort. Anim., vi, 10.
[5] De Ord., ii, 2.

the senses. They appear to him to be mean when compared with the nobler nature of the intellect. They may even prove dangerous because they are the ultimate source of the *Imagines*, which hinder true knowledge. Their products are liable to confusion with the latter, and in such cases this is a great misfortune.[1]

Nature of Sense Perception

The ancients in general did not clearly distinguish between sensation and sense perception and Woerter[2] points out that this is a feature in the writings of Augustine.

In the course of a long discussion on sense perception in *De Quant. Anim.*, xxiii. Augustine defines senses as "non latere animam quod patitur corpus." Later, however, Augustine realises that this definition is too wide. By means of deduction the mind is aware of the growth of the hair and finger nails, and does not reach this knowledge of growth by direct sensation or perception. The formula, therefore, is made more accurate. Perception is that which through itself (per se ipsam) does not escape the mind. The term "non latere animam" is not equivalent to knowledge, otherwise we should have to attribute knowledge to the animals. "Non latere animam" is common to both "scientia" and "sensus," although the latter differ. This difference becomes clear when it is said that what does not escape the mind per Rationem is knowledge. The animal has no Ratio, no Mens; the animal has only the "vis sentiendi"; man possesses the "vis sciendi" also. Sense perception the animal has;

---

[1] *Cont. Acad.*, iii, 6.

[2] *Die Unsterblichkeitslehre in den philosophischen Schriften Augustins.* Freiburg. 1880.

his senses are five in number, and some of these are superior to what they are in the human being.

External Sense
(a) Vision

Augustine, like Plato and Plotinus, regards sight as the noblest sense. Vision is the faculty of the eye, and shines out upon that which is perceived, and so it is clear that vision takes place where the object is and not where vision appears to proceed from. In the act of vision it may be said that I see a person, although I am not where the person is. If the eye saw just where the eye itself is, it would only see itself. Consequently it is only possible for the eye to see where it is not and likewise it receives, or is sensitive there where it is not ("ibi eos pati ubi non sunt").

The fact that the organs of the body are subject to those diseases and that suffering to which the body is liable, suggests that sense perception must be assigned to the bodily part of the constitution, and not to the higher intellectual part, like phantasia. A sense organ may be more effectual in proportion to the smallness of its bulk. For Augustine, that which has no bulk at all is the ideal.

Young children had a keener sense of perception in proportion as their share of reason is less; they are quick to distinguish their nurse by touch and smell.[1] This statement of Augustine, however, is not psychologically true. Knowledge is denied to animals, even the "sense-knowledge" of human beings. Animal perception is "sentire" not "scire."[2]

Deduction is a process, in which both sense-perception and the Intellect have each a part. A person deduces the

---

[1] De Quant. Anim., xxviii, 54.
[2] De Quant. Anim., xv, 26.

presence of fire when seeing smoke. The activity in this process is that of the mind, but the material worked upon is that of sense perception and therefore this particular kind of activity is termed knowledge through the senses ("cognitio per sensum vocatur.")[1]

In *Conf.*, vii, 10, Augustine writes: "And Thou didst counteract the weakness of my sight, streaming forth Thy beams of light upon me most fully." According to ancient psychology, the eye projected a pencil of rays of light towards its object. These rays Augustine here conceives as meeting, and being beaten back by the rays of the light unapproachable in which God dwells.[2]

In *De Gen. ad Litt.*, i, 31, Augustine refers to the psychological fact that when the eye is specially directed to an object in the foreground, distant objects are seen more dimly than when we look directly at them from the same position. He illustrates some experiments he made in closing one eye.[3] He also speaks of the effect of closing the eyes after viewing some bright object and reference to vision by deflecting the eyeballs and also in then experiencing an after-image of the object with the eyes closed, which is clearly an impress on the sense.

He also speaks in *De Trin.*, xi of the act of will which is required in directing the sense-organ towards its object and keeping it focussed on it.

(b) Nature of Sound

Augustine, when speaking of God's word at the Creation, uses such phrases as "verberatus aer," "aere percusso"; he argues that he does not mean a word

[1] *De Quant. Anim.*, xxiv, 45.
[2] I Tim. vi, 6.
[3] *De Trin.*, xi, 4.

literally, because there was no medium by which it could be transmitted.[1]

In *De Mus.*, vi, 21, Augustine emphasises the fact that memory is operative in acts of hearing; he illustrates this remark by explaining that, when speaking a word of two syllables, the listener retains in the memory the first syllable until the second is heard. If this were not so the word would not be comprehended as a whole. Even in a lesser degree, this is true with a word of one syllable, where memory must retain the first part of the syllable till the last is uttered.

(c) Sense of Smell

In *Ep.*, 137, 6, he says that it may perhaps be reasonably disputed whether the sense of smell is perceived by direct contact or not. He, however, thinks it is by direct contact and he seems to hold the modern opinion that bodies which emit odour discharge into the atmosphere infinitely minute particles which come into contact with and excite the olfactory nerves.

Impressions to the Inner Man

In *De Magistro*, a letter or discussion which Augustine wrote to Adeodatus his son, he describes the impression which signs convey to our senses. He points out, however, that this is after all an external impression, although impressions are really conveyed to the inner man. There is also a teacher within and that teacher is Christ. Augustine here refers to *Eph.* iii, 16, 17: "Strengthened by his Spirit in the inner man, that Christ may dwell in your hearts through faith." Christ is, he points out, the power of God and the Eternal Wisdom, on whom every

[1] *Cf. De Vera Relig.*, 79; *De Mus.*, vi, 11; *Conf.*, xi, 8.

rational soul depends. Everything depends on the teacher of the inner man. In the sphere of mental conceptions we are conscious of ideas by means of the light of truth, by which the inner man is enlightened. If I speak what is true, the hearer is not taught merely by any words, but by the realities which they suggest clearly to him, especially through the light which God bestows.

Self Examination

We have in the *Soliloquies* a brief but extraordinary comprehensive prayer that is characteristic of the great writer's deeply religious spirit: "God Who art always the same, let me know myself, let me know Thee." ("Deus semper idem, noverim me, noverim Te. Oratum est.")

The *self-analysis* of Augustine is extraordinarily minute. It embraces also an inquiry into the gradual growth of the life of sense. He refers to the innate sinful tendency which displays itself even in infancy. "Where or when," he asks, "was I innocent?" He frequently reminds us of Pascal in the tone of his reflections on the helplessness, misery, and nothingness of man, his blindness and incapacity in face of the problems confronting him, the toilsomeness of the search after truth, the narrow range of the perceptive faculties, the poverty (inopia) which besets his powers whether of investigation or of expression.[1]

Augustine's *view of man's nature* is the fruit of prolonged self-scrutiny. We may remark that he departs from the psychology of his time, such as it was, in emphasising the importance of will rather than of intellect as the essence and inmost reality of personality. To him his fellow-men are "nihil aliud quam voluntates." Just as in the Godhead

[1] xii, 1, 1; R. L. Ottley. *The Confessions of St. Augustine*, p. 94.

itself: "Voluntas Dei et potentia Deus ipse est."[1] So in human nature the will is the man. Christianity is before everything else a *life*, a putting forth of victorious and organising energy, and it was precisely here that Augustine knew himself to have failed. He was not the man he aspired to be just in so far as his will was weak and enslaved by sinful habit. He recognised that the life of fellowship with God necessarily had its root in man's dedication of his will to goodness. Augustine's conversion consisted in this: "nolle quod volebam, velle quod volebas."[2] His self-analysis in fact taught him that the appeal of truth is made not primarily to reason or to emotion but to will. He would adopt for himself the prayer uttered by St. Paul on behalf of his Ephesian converts: that "the eyes of their heart"—the seat of will and affection—"may be enlightened that they may know the things of God."[3]

St. Augustine anticipated modern thought so far as to formulate his ideas on the subject of psycho-analysis, in reference to which he developed a remarkable philosophy.

Memory and Understanding

In his analysis of all mankind, he emphasises memory as the primary spiritual faculty in man, and the foundation of all rational life. It never occurred to him that memory must ever seek to purify itself by trying to forget. In his theory and practice, it is naturally purified by the understanding, which is the next in order of the human faculties. Memory retains everything indiscriminately, good and

[1] *Conf.*, vii, 4, 6.
[2] lx, 11.
[3] Eph., i, 18.

M

evil, truth and falsehood, phantasms and sensations. The understanding interprets all of them, recognising only goodness and truth as realities, and showing evil to be naught, phantasms and sensations almost naught—hence the fascinating play of optimism and pessimism which has been frequently noted in Augustine's writings and in the Christian culture which dates from him, but which is absent from all pagan culture. The delight of pagans in fancies and sensations is never changed to wistful tears by the discovery that they are naught.[1]

Augustine's supposition that he was an ordinary man died with him, but his psychological theory of common manhood continued unquestioned for eight hundred years until Thomas Aquinas, his greatest and most devoted disciple, equal to him in the power of memory, superior in understanding, rejected it.

Instincts

Instincts are innate mental dispositions which are common to all the members of any one species. They play a large part in regulating the behaviour of the lower animals; so far as man is influenced by instincts, they are an inheritance from his animal ancestry. Instincts are inherited and are not acquired during the individual's own life-time; they must, therefore be distinguished from habit. The instinct of self-preservation appears clearly to be connected not only with what has been termed the Providence element in religion—an element which looks to God as the provider for our immediate needs—but also with man's desire for immortality.[2]

[1] J. Reeves in *A Monument to St. Augustine*, p. 137.
[2] See Thouless. *Introduction to the Psychology of Religion*, p. 126.

It is also connected with those self-interested tendencies which come into conflict with the requirements of religious society. The sex-instinct is similarly connected with the desire for a worthy object of love and a giver of love; the gregarious instinct results in a high value being placed on the social group as compared with the individual; this results in a sentiment which centres in the Church and in the religious individual's respect for traditional authority.

The influence of an instinct on the mind always begins and ends in relation to an object of the external world. It is first excited by that object, and then certain mental activities take place in regard to the object. This is followed by action taking place with reference to the object. Three mental processes are thus involved—the cognitive, the affective and the conative. In cognition the mind knows or takes cognisance of the object; the affective aspect appears when a specific emotion is awakened; conation is the mental effort towards appropriate action.

Intellectual Desires

Augustine concentrates on the study of the higher intellectual desires. He tells us that his one great desire was to know the soul and God. In *De Beata Vita* he discusses the relation of a mere search after God and Blessedness. He asks whether the mere search for God, irrespective of whether we find Him or not, brings happiness. He argues that the man who seeks Him finds God already propitious to him and therefore he is blessed, even though he has not what he seeks. The wise man will direct his mind and his wishes only to contemplate things which he can get. He raises himself above need by the exercise of his will. Freedom from need is the essence of happiness and is identified with "Sapientia."[1]

Admiration

In *Conf.*, iv, 14, Augustine mentions what may be called a psychological difficulty as to the different kinds of admiration. "Do I then love in a man, what I, who am a man, hate to be?" Augustine believes that in admiring an actor or gladiator he is considering him merely as a means to his own enjoyment and not from the standpoint of dignity of human nature.

Weeping (Physico-Psychology)

In *Conf.*, iv, 5, Augustine suggests that the sensation of weeping harmonises with painful emotion, and thus gives that measure of satisfaction which is afforded by the appropriate expression of feeling: "Or is weeping indeed a bitter thing, and caused by very loathing of the things, which we before enjoyed? Does it then, when we shrink in disgust from them, please us?"

In this he approaches the modern physico-psychological explanation that weeping relieves the painful tension which is set up by the reaction of emotion on the physical organism.[2]

Crowd Psychology

It has been the custom of many writers to treat of the psychology of the crowd as if it were essentially different from the psychology of the individual, and to refer to imitation or suggestibility as if it were almost created by the presence of the mob. Yet the human nature of an

---

[1] *De Beat. Vit.*, iv, 33.

[2] Gibb and Montgomery. *The Confessions of Augustine*, p. 89.

individual in a crowd is the same as elsewhere, and there are not really two systems of psychology, the individual and the social. As has been pointed out by Professor Pratt,[1] the acts which men perform when in association with others are the result of the same fundamental forces that control their action when alone. What the presence of a crowd does is to emphasise certain factors already present, which it is able to do because of man's peculiar sensitiveness to social stimuli. It does not create suggestibility, but it does increase it. This it does in two ways: (1) by weakening or banishing all inhibitory tendencies, and also (2) by increasing the dominance over attention possessed by the central idea or impulse. These are, of course, but two aspects of the same thing, but they are usually considered separately.

Augustine gives a striking example of crowd psychology in *Conf.*, xi, 8. He is referring to a friend, Alypius by name, who at one time was a lover of gladiatorial shows but had renounced them, and for years had kept away from them. He was persuaded to visit a show by his friends and was carried away by the enthusiasm of the crowd and again became devoted to this special type of cruelty. Augustine says of him: "Nor was he now the man who had come thither, but one of the crowd to which he had come ("Unus de turba"), and was intoxicated with the bloody pastime."

The account is a vivid piece of writing combining graphic descriptions with keen psychological analysis. Crowds have a kind of personality which every member of the crowd shares.[2]

Another illustration of crowd psychology is seen in

[1] *The Religious Consciousness*, p. 171.
[2] Gibb and Montgomery. *The Confessions of Augustine*, p. 153.

Conf., x, 35, where he gives an account of a crowd drawn together to see a mangled body.

Augustine also gives an illustration of the sympathy between speaker and audience in *De Catech. Rud.*, 17. He instances the difficulty of a teacher constantly teaching the same elementary lesson to pupils who may find such tuition wearisome. If, on the other hand, he teaches with a father's love, a sympathetic disposition will arise and he will feel himself in touch with his pupil.

Child Psychology.

In *De Trin.*, xiv, 7, Augustine refers to a certain instinct of an infant to see the light, and in other passages, *De Civ. Dei*, xiii, 3, and *De Quant. Anim.*, liv, he records other details concerning child life. In the former passage he speaks of the prolonged helplessness of the child compared with the lower animals and suggests that this is in proportion to its ultimate higher efficiency. He uses the following apt illustration in connection with his remarks: "As an arrow has to be drawn further back the further it is to shoot." In *Conf.* i, 8, he explains how a child learns to speak, not so much by rules as by the gesture and words of his parents.

In *Conf.* i, 6, we have a characteristically accurate statement of minute psychological observation. Speaking of his childhood Augustine writes: "Afterwards I began to smile; first in sleep, then waking." His child-psychology is first-hand, as he tells us: "Such have I learnt infants to be from observing them: and that I was myself such, they, all unconscious, have shown me better than my nurses who knew it."[1]

[1] *Ibid.*

Internal Sense

The soul is conscious of its own activity through the operation of the internal sense and by reason. The soul contemplates these things which are intelligible by its higher faculty, that is to say by reason and by intelligence. To have an intuition of intelligible things, it is sufficient if it concentrates on these. Intellectual intuition is analogous to the intuition which is the result of the operation of the senses.

"Ideae," "formae," "species," "notiones" are identical with the divine intelligence. Contemplation on these illuminates human intelligence. This contemplation is common to all men.

The special senses are presided over, according to Augustine, by what he calls the "internal sense" ("interior sensus"), to which he says[1] the special senses make their report—"cui sensus corporis exteriora nuntiunt." It also judges whether the sense-organ is functioning properly or not.[2]

The "interior sensus" appears to be simply consciousness so far as it is concerned with sensation, and it is not quite clear why these functions should be assigned to a special faculty. These powers are also enjoyed by animals and therefore we cannot designate them as "reason," and so Augustine assigns these functions to the "interior sensus." This division of Augustine's does not appear to be entirely satisfactory, for the simple reason that above the "interior sensus" Augustine classifies memory and imagination; as animals enjoy memory we cannot altogether exclude them as devoid of an "interior sensus."

[1] Conf., vii, 23.
[2] De Lib. Arb., ii, 12.

This "interior sensus" which correlates sensations (*a*) with each other, and (*b*) with the self as the subject of sensation, must be regarded as equivalent to the Aristotelian "commonsense." Augustine's teaching on the "interior sensus" differs widely from that of Plato. It follows the philosophy of Aristotle. The latter relates the sense organs to each other by a means of common or central sense.[1] Wallace thinks that it was probably in a spirit of antagonism to the teaching of Plato that Aristotle referred the common categories which enter into our perceptions to the sensitive faculty itself, and not to the soul or mind directly, as Plato does.

In *De Lib. Arbit.*, ii, 3, 4, 5, Augustine takes pains to work out a conception concerning the " interior sensus " for himself. He does not refer to Aristotle. It is probable that the latter's theory was familiar to all the members of the Stoic and Neo-Platonic Schools of philosophy. This central sense as a perceptive faculty stands to each one of the separate senses, as the mind stands to each of its faculties. It has two functions, the distinction and comparison of the messages of the single senses, and also the supplying of the consciousness which accompanies the act of perception.[2] Aristotle takes pains to show that it must be "sensus," and not "ratio," which does this work, for the qualities to be compared are objects of the senses. The "interior sensus" gives also the consciousness of sensation, i.e. by means of it we know a sensation is ours. The seat of the "interior sensus" was placed by Aristotle in the heart.

Augustine, on the other hand, localises the seat of function in the brain. In *De Gen. ad Litt.*, xxiv, he tells

[1] Wallace. *Aristotle's Psychology*. Cambridge, 1882.
[2] *De Anim.*, iii, 2 ,10.

us that there are three "ventricles," so to speak, of the brain, the anterior, which has to do with the senses, the posterior, which has to do with all movement, and the third, or central, portion in which memory is located. He states that physicians assert that disease or injury to one or other of these portions is accompanied by disturbance or suspension of one or other of these functions. The physicians, referred to by Augustine, are on the track of an important psychological truth in thus localising function.

Observation

It is in reference to that aspect of psychology which concerns observation that Augustine reveals his greatness. There is nothing very remarkable about his system, his classification of mental powers and so forth; it is an eclectic system drawn from various sources. He possessed a very remarkable power of introspection and extraordinary skill in recording his observations. He does not merely give vivid descriptions of religious feelings; his observations on general psychology are such as to evoke the admiration of modern experts on the subject.

What he received through the medium of the ear and eye provided him with a wealth of imagery wherewith to illustrate the inner life.[1]

His great power of psychological observation leads him to views of paedagogy which we are apt to think of as modern.[2] "It is quite clear then, that a free curiosity has more force in our learning these things than a terrifying enforcement."[3] His dialogues with his pupils

[1] Gibb and Montgomery. *The Confessions of Augustine*, p. 318.
[2] *Cf. Conf.*, i, 14.
[3] *De Magistro, Cont. Acad., De Ord.*, etc.

indicate that he followed the method of stimulating and guiding the "libera curiositas" with much success.

Interior Illumination

Augustine's doctrine of interior illumination shows that he believes the light of the Word to be the unique source which clarifies all knowledge. From a psychological point of view, no doubt, we thus have a primary knowledge of ourselves which disposes us to seek God; but, in a still more profoundly true perspective, our illusions with regard to ourselves, the meaning of our existence and the destiny of our being, appear to us only through an illuminating knowledge of God. So, not only from a speculative but also from a moral and religious point of view, he repeats and exemplifies the doctrine that to know himself a man must know God, regard God, so to speak, as within himself, and discovering Him in his own image: "Noverim me, noverim Te."[1]

Affective-tone

It may be said that Augustine divides "the feelings" into two classes—organic and intellectual. In reference to the former it is evident that animals, as well as men, experience certain feelings of pleasure and pain which arise from different states of the organism. Some change in the organism is caused by an alteration in their surroundings. Augustine does not provide us with any analysis of the feelings. There are numerous references to animal psychology in his writings, but these are set forth, as a rule, to institute comparisons and to suggest illustrations. He refers to insects, and even to the

1 M. Blondel. *A Monument to St. Augustine*, p. 331.

dissection of them, but the subject of feelings is not treated of.

The animal world is in a higher grade than that of the insect world. The animal is governed by its feelings in reference to its behaviour towards the outer world.

(a) *Pain*

In *De Libero Arbitrio* Augustine discusses the resemblance (ordained by the Creator) of the animal to the human soul in the matter of pain. He refers to the significance of pain and explains that it is a danger signal of division in the organism and a shrinking away from it.[1] The soul strives instinctively to preserve the harmony and the integrity of the organs in all their parts, and pain is the alarm signal at the appearance of any threatened division. The pain which animals suffer exhibits a certain sensibility of the animal soul and thus it becomes ennobling. It shows, at the same time, a certain power ("Vim") in the animal soul.[2] ("Dolor autem quem bestiae sentirent, animarum etiam bestialium vim quamdam in suo genere mirabilem, laudabilemque commendat.") As regards man, however, bodily pain is of all things the worst, for it hinders the pursuit of knowledge.[3]

Augustine's view of pain is seen in a different aspect in *De Ordine*. Whereas in *De Libero Arbitrio* it is regarded, from a teleological standpoint as a good, because it warns of division and the need of attention, in the latter treatise it is regarded as the agent of division itself and is an unmixed evil. The principle of Oneness is essential to all real existence and consequently the disintegrating

---

[1] *De Lib. Arb.*, iii, 23.
[2] *De Lib. Arb.*, iii, 23.
[3] *Solil.*, i, 12.

nature of pain must be regarded as the root of its evil character.[1]

(b) Pleasure

Pleasure, as the antithesis of pain, delights in the harmony of elements which strive towards closer unity with one another. In *De Beata Vita* joy appears to belong pre-eminently to the soul. This joy is greater in proportion as the soul disentangles itself from the body. Augustine distinguishes between joy and mirth. The latter has no place in animal psychology, but it occupies the lowest levels in the life of man.[2]

(c) Conation—Desire and Will

Augustine has no developed theory of the connection between feelings, on the one hand, and desires and will on the other. It is doubtful whether he has really in his mind any clear view of the distinction between desire and will. He asks "Quid amor omnis?"[3] and he appears to include in his meaning of the term both desires and impulses arising from the direction of the body. Thus desire is motived impulse, and its aim is to draw the subject and the object of desire within the bounds of unity, conceived of as the characteristic of the Universe.

Augustine specially emphasises the love of existence as commendable because it is directed towards Veritas and in possessing this desire the individual approximates to the fountain of existence which is God.[4]

In contradiction to the love of existence, Augustine

---

[1] *De Ord.*, ii, 18.
[2] *De Lib. Arb.*, i, 8.
[3] *De Ord.* ii, 18.
[4] *De Lib. Arb.*, iii, 7.

points out the hatefulness of taking one's own life.[1] The motive of suicides is that they think they will either be going to a better place or that they will cease to exist, but Augustine thinks that no suicide has non-existence in view.[2]

Bodily desires or lusts rob man of freedom, and man is liable to be governed by the lusts. Man's world becomes a Cosmos only when these desires are all subordinated to the reason.[3] Augustine shows a certain independence of the teaching of Plato and asserts that the possession of reason does not necessarily guarantee power over oneself. Although a person may conquer wild beasts yet he may be powerless to subdue himself.[4] Fools are such, not because they are devoid of reason, but because they do not submit to its rule. He also points out that Ratio is stronger than desire and passion. Plato pays little attention generally to the impulses.[5] Augustine does not fail to estimate the strength of appetite.

Some examples of emotion mentioned by Augustine may be found in the following passages of his treatises.

Augustine, when mourning the death of a friend writes: "By this grief, my heart was utterly darkened, and whenever I looked I saw naught but death .... I became a great enigma to myself, and I asked my soul, why she was so sad, and why she disquieted me sorely ... tears were my only comfort, for they took my friend's place in the dearest of my affections.[6]

---

[1] *De Lib. Arb.*, iii, 8.
[2] T. J. Parry. *Augustine and Platonism*, p. 29.
[3] *De Lib. Arb.*, i, 8; *Solil.*, i, 9.
[4] *De Lib. Arb.*, i, 9.
[5] Siebeck. *Geschichte der Psychologie* I, 1, p. 228.
[6] *Conf.*, iv, 9.

Augustine's meaning appears to be that the painful sensation of weeping harmonises with the painful emotion, and thus provides that satisfaction which is afforded by the appropriate expression of feeling.

Augustine had inherited the gift of tears from his mother. As a child he had wept over the *Aeneid*. As an adolescent he wept about the misfortunes of lovers, and his return to Christ was destined to culminate in a flood of tears.

In *Conf.*, vi, 16, it appears that Augustine was tormented by a fear of death and judgment to come. He describes it as a fear that was always present in his breast.

In *Conf.*, ix, 12, we read that Augustine, on the death of his mother, attempted to suppress all manifestations of grief, holding it to be unbecoming in a Christian. Even at the graveside he suppresses his emotion, but when alone he is unable any longer to restrain his tears. In the passage in which he records his last conversation with his mother at Ostia, there is an attempt to describe an experience similar to an ecstasy in the Neo-Platonic sense.

Certitude[1]

In order to rescue himself, says Erdmann, from the scepticism of the Academy, St. Augustine seeks for an immovable basis of all knowledge, and finds this in self-confidence, with which a thinking being asserts his own existence. This remains certain in spite of all doubts, and indeed, becomes certain through them. From this

[1] Dr. Tennant (*Philosophical Theology*, vol. I. p. 290) distinguishes between "Certitude" and "Certainty" and points out that the term "certitude" should be used for describing a state of mind—the conviction such as is affirmed by the statement: "I am certain that. . . ."; the term "certainty," on the other hand, is employed to describe the objective character ascribed to propositions independently of whether they are believed, as in the statement "it is certain that. . . ."

starting-point, which he asserts to be incontrovertible, in particularly in the *Soliloquia*,[1] in *De Libero Arbitrio*,[2] and *De Vera Religione*,[3] he proceeds, especially in the second work mentioned, to distinguish in this self assurance, certainty of being, of life, of feeling, and of rational perception, and thus gives it a fourfold content. . . . Everywhere belief is the beginning. In so far, belief and authority go before reason. This, however, is true only in respect to chronological order; judged according to their worth, knowledge and insight stand higher.[4] [5]

From Augustine's first certitude, his doctrine at once leads to further consequences. Not only his religious conviction, but also a deep epistemological reflection enables him to regard the idea of God as immediately involved in the certainty, which the individual consciousness has of itself.

In his philosophy Augustine starts from the principle of the immediate certainty of knowledge. Even doubt cannot but testify to the fact of knowledge. Thence he proceeds to show that the existence of God is necessarily involved in this first principle. With these two normative principles he has a firm basis, and finds himself able to unite the individual and the universal. Proceeding to expand the conception of Deity, Augustine at once reveals his ability as a master of interpretation by adopting the will as the central characteristic.

How can we question and doubt, asks this great thinker, the perceptions of the external world, which impress themselves upon us with such elementary force, if we did not enjoy, in addition to these, and from other

[1] ii, 1. [2] ii, 7. [3] 72
[4] *De Util. Cred.*, ix, 21, 16, 31; *De Ord.*, ii, 9, 26.
[5] *Hist. of Philos.* Translation. Vol. I, p. 272.

sources, certain criteria and canons of truth, by means of which we can examine and measure these perceptions?

In *Contra Academicos*, iii, 11, Augustine states that it is in vain that anyone engages in argument against the certainty of knowledge from the standpoint of particular states of the soul, which are called sleep, or folly, or even from that which is called the errors of the senses. It is certainly in ourselves, in the immediate intuition of the soul, independently of external events, and outside the sphere of changes, that certitude, which is the basis of knowledge, is found.[1]

St. Augustine lays great emphasis on the fact that even the sceptic, who denies the external reality of the content of perception, or, at least, leaves it undecided, cannot remain in doubt about the internal existence of the sensation as such.

From this basis, he advances to victorious certainty. He asserts that together with the sensation, something else is given in addition to its content. Its content is liable to doubt in one direction or another. It is necessary to postulate the reality of the perceiving subject.

From the very act of doubt, the certainty, which consciousness has of itself, follows. Augustine asserts, as Descartes did in different terms at a later period: "Because I doubt, I know that I, the doubter, exist." Again, he writes in *De Civ. Dei*, xi, 27: "In my inner man, I both am, and know that I am; and I love both being and knowledge, and I know that I love them both." In *De Civ. Dei*, xi, 26, he also says: "I know with certainty that I am, and that I know and love my own existence." It is this self-consciousness that he adopts as the basis or starting-point of thought for his metaphysics in psychology.

[1] *De Div. Quaest.*, lxiii, 30.

It is just this doubt, expressed in the first of these passages, which contains within itself the valuable truth of the reality of the conscious being. The climax to this system of reasoning is rather remarkable, for Augustine is willing to state that, even if he should err in all else, he cannot err in this; for, in order to err, he must exist.

This line of argument was regarded as most important by Augustine and he frequently employs it in developing his theories.[1] This kind of argument was not altogether unknown in Greek literature. This fact is proved by a passage of an unfinished work, which has received the title of *Metaphysics of Herennios*.[2]

St. Augustine recognises that this fundamental certainty applies equally to all states of consciousness. He even endeavours to show that all these various states are already included in the act of doubt.

St. Augustine is certain that he who doubts knows, not only that he lives, but also that he remembers, that he knows, and that he wills. When we endeavour to ascertain by analysis, what are the grounds of his doubt, we discover that they rest upon his former ideas. We learn that, while we are estimating the momentia of the doubt, thought, knowledge, and judgment are developed.

Where shall we locate the basis of certitude? Neither in accordance with tradition, nor universal consent, nor according to simple experience was Augustine willing to formulate his unshaken foundation. Contemplating the lowest depths of the soul, he asserted that the consciousness of his being and of his mode of being was revealed in his belief of life and that it was in the fact of his thought

[1] *De Trin.*, x, 14; *De Ver. Relig.*, 78; *Sol.*, ii, 1; *De Beata Vita*, 7.
[2] iii, 6.

N

that he discovered the fact of certitude surrounded by an irresistible light.

"We are, we know that we are, and we love our being and the knowledge that we have of it. No illusion is possible about these three objects. . . . I am very certain that, independent of all phantasy and illusion of the imagination, I myself exist, that I know and that I love my being."[1]

After all, the motive of his doubt is only that he is striving after truth. There is no necessity to reflect upon this fact at too great length, nor need we draw further conclusions from it. It is sufficient at this juncture to mention that Augustine proves by this statement his deep insight into the psychical life, inasmuch as he does not regard the different kinds of psychical activity as separate spheres (cognition, feeling, will), but as the aspects of one and the same act, and inseparably united with one another.

St. Augustine's argument on the subject of the Reality of the conscious nature or essence is most important. The self-certainty of the soul was valued by him as the most convincing of all experiences, as the fundamental fact of inner perception, by means of which the latter obtains for the theory of knowledge a greater degree of authority than outer perception.

Seeking, in opposition to Scepticism, an indubitable certitude as a point of departure for all philosophical investigation, St. Augustine finds it, as appears in his work *Contra Academicos*, in all disjunctive propositions on the one hand, and he remarks, on the other, that our sensible perceptions are at least subjectively true. "Noli, plus assentiri quam ut ita tibi apparere persuadeas, et

[1] *De Civ. Dei*, xi, 26.

nulla deceptio est."[1] In another of his works, Augustine lays down the principle, which has been so fruitful in philosophy, that it is impossible to doubt one's own existence.[2] The philosophical system of Descartes begins with universal methodic doubt; the famous "cogito, ergo sum," on which the whole system is based, suggests the solution of the philosopher's fundamental doubt of his own existence. This solution was anticipated by St. Augustine, who took the subjective certainty of one's own existence as the ground of all certainty: "Tuqui vis te nosse, scis esse te? Scio. Unde scis? Nescio. Cogitare te scis? Scio."[3] [4]

The irresistible force of the internal consciousness, the conviction of feeling, in Augustine's case, fused with the penetrating light of the intellect. But few enjoy this gift in such perfection. The great importance of St. Augustine's teaching centres in the fact that he recognised the necessity of tracing the unrest of the believing or seeking soul to its roots, and of making sure of the inner facts, by which the heart can reach its rest.

Perception and Cognition

Augustine's "Ideology" appears at its best in *De Gen. ad Litt.*, xii. It is primarily concerned with St. Paul's vision of the "third heaven." Augustine lays down certain governing principles which include ordinary perception and cognition. He distinguishes three kinds of perception, according to the three kinds of objects perceived. He speaks of Corporal or Liberal perception,

---

[1] *Cont. Acad.*, iii, 26.
[2] *De Beat. Vit.*, vii.
[3] *Sol.* ii, 1.
[4] See also *De Trin.*, x, 14.

by which physical things are seen; Spiritual or Imaginative perception, whereby are seen images of physical things not present, as in memory and imagination; Intellectual perception, whereby are seen things incapable of being represented by images, such as objects of the pure intellect. This he would term "mental."[1]

Augustine illustrates his theory by referring to the case of one reading the commandment: "Thou shalt love thy neighbour as thyself." The actual letters are seen by the bodily eye, i.e. corporeal perception; the absent neighbour is seen with the mind's eye, i.e. spiritual or imaginary perception; and "love" refers to intellectual perception.

Augustine usually conjoins corporal and spiritual perception as both are the perception of changeable things, and therefore the objects of science ("scientia"), as distinguished from wisdom (sapientia), whereby are perceived things not subject to change and eternal. Elsewhere he distinguishes wisdom and science: "To wisdom pertains the intellectual cognition of things eternal; to science the rational cognition of things temporal."[2]

In corporal and spiritual (imaginary) perception the soul is liable to error; but in things intellectually seen it is not; if there be any error, it is because the soul does not intellectually see, for things intellectually seen are truly seen.[3] Augustine terms the objects of intellectual vision "intelligibilia" and "intellectualia" indiscriminately, saying that the attempt to make a distinction would be too subtle a process.[4]

As objects of pure intellectual perception he enumerates

[1] xii, 6–9.
[2] De Trin., xii, 25.
[3] De Gen. ad Litt., xii, 25; also xii, 14.
[4] De Gen. ad Litt., xii, 10.

the mind itself, every good disposition (affectio) of the soul, or virtue, e.g. charity, joy, peace, and the rest, by which it draws near to God, and, lastly, God Himself.[1]

In *De Trin.*, xii, 23, he discourses about "intelligibilia." To wisdom pertain those things that neither have been nor are to be, but are; and because of that eternity in which they exist, they are said to have been, to be, and to be about to be, without any change of time; they always have had the selfsame being, and they always have it. They abide, not fixed in local spaces like bodies, but in an incorporeal nature "intelligibilia" are as present to the gate of the mind as visible and tangible things in places are present to the bodily senses. The "rationes" of sensible things existing in place, continue to be intelligible and incorporeal, but not in local spaces; the squareness of a square figure abides as an incorporeal and unchangeable "ratio."

About intellectual vision, Augustine sometimes speaks in the same vague way of the light wherein "intellectualia" or "intelligibilia," the Platonic "Ideas," are believed to be: It is to be believed that the nature of the intellectual mind has been so fashioned, that when brought into contact (subjuncta) with "intelligibilia" in the natural order, by the disposition of the Creator, it sees them in a certain incorporeal light "sui generis," as the eye of the flesh sees the things around in this corporeal light.[2]

In *De Gen. ad Litt.*, xii, it is emphasised that in intellectual vision the light wherein the soul sees all truly intellectual objects (omnia veraciter intellectua) is God Himself.

[1] *De Gen. ad Litt.*, xii, 24.
[2] *De Trin.*, xii, 24.

It is evident, according to the teaching of Augustine, that the human mind perceives "ideas," "intelligibilia," in some way in the Light of God, and understands all verity in the Truth unchangeable, which is God. Therefore his Ideology, or theory of how the mind comes to the knowledge of "intelligibilia," is the doctrine of divine illumination. This teaching, as the result of the influence of St. Augustine's authority, prevailed in the early Middle Ages, until it was generally supplanted by that of Aristotle on the subject as expanded by Thomas Aquinas. It was perpetuated in the Franciscan school of St. Bonaventura, and Thomas Aquinas admitted it to be quite tenable and quite probable.

Memory

Memory has been termed the fundamental phenomenon of mental operations. Some psychologists describe an elementary memory and an implicate memory. The former is the immediate interaction among successive sensations, the latter is the memory conditioning the percept "implicate." It is possible for an implicate memory to be changed into a free memory. Psychology inquires into the conditions necessary for retention of ideas. It also investigates such subjects as memory, image, hallucinations and remembrance of feelings.

Free memory image is distinct not only from the immediate percept and from the immediate after-effects of sensations, but also from certain representations which emerge without external cause—the so-called hallucinations. Hallucinations arise, like percepts, with the appearance of reality, and it is often difficult, if not impossible, for an individual to distinguish them from actual percepts. In this respect there are many differences of degree. In dream-images the actual impressions received during sleep play so important a part that the images may be classed rather as illusions than as hallucinations.

Hallucinations, like the memory image, are sometimes produced voluntarily. They are sometimes memory-images, which suddenly adopt the appearance of reality.

Feelings are remembered by means of the ideas with which they were originally linked, and in conjunction with which they caused a certain conscious state to arise.

Memory may be described as an ideational process, so far as it assumes the form of the reproduction and recognition of prior experiences in their original time order. Memory may be said to include the three relatively distinguishable functions of Reproduction, Recognition, and Localisation.

Plato failed to distinguish between memory proper and retentiveness in general. Hobbes defines both memory and imagination, including all mental imagery, as "decaying sense." The word memory is used to indicate that the mental image presupposes a primary experience, which it revives. The word imagination is used to indicate that the revival is relatively faint, or, as Hobbes would say, "decayed."

It has always been admitted that in the treatment of memory Augustine employs his special gifts to advantage. He places memory in the ascending order of the powers of the soul, immediately above the inner sense. The chief passage in his writings which treats of this subject is in *Confessions*, x. In this chapter we find many statements which singularly remind us of the language of Locke in his *An Essay concerning Human Understanding*. "I pass from those natural powers," Augustine says, "which have been implanted in me for the purpose of exalting me, as by degrees, towards Him Who has created me, and I arrive at certain vast tracts of country and those palaces of memory, in which are enshrined the treasures of an infinite number of images, which have found an entrance through the avenues of sensation."

"When I arrive at these plains of memory, I make the request that certain ideas, which I desire, should appear, and suddenly some ideas arise in my mind, but others require a longer search and make their appearance slowly as if they were drawn forth with difficulty from the depths of a hidden cavern; others make their appearance in a crowd, and even those which I am not searching for make their appearance." Here the writer clearly teaches the doctrine of "association of ideas." St. Augustine, says Sir William Hamilton, reduces association to a single canon, viz., "Thoughts, which have once co-existed in the mind, are afterwards associated."[1] "There are other ideas," he says, "which, without leaving the series, come forth, with facility in the same order as I wish."

Another statement of Augustine, also, resembles the teaching of Locke. "In the same treasure-house of my memory, I preserve distinctly and without any confusion all percepts, which, according to their different natures have entered there, each by the avenue which is suitable, as the light, etc. . . . This great storehouse of memory remains open to receive all these perceptions, for the purpose of bringing them forth to us, when we have need of them."

It is important to remember that Augustine uses the word "memory" with a somewhat varied sense of meaning. It refers to the present as much as to the past;

[1] *Metaphysics* II, 231.

it emphasises his belief that within the soul resides knowledge and truth. In one passage he describes memory thus: "the memory, then, is as it were the belly of the mind."[1]

The things perceived by the mind are perceived as ever present in the light of that eternal, inner light of the mind. It is the inner eye of the mind which sees and illumines those truths which already exist in the mind.

Ignorance is no proof that these truths are not already existent. The ignorant person suffers from some inherent weakness (imbecillitate) which disables him from using that inner light of the mind, and from guiding it, as it were, in the direction of these innate truths.

In *De Quant. Anim.*, xx, Augustine expresses with great decision, his belief in the doctrine of Innate ideas. The mind has brought everything with it from the pre-existent state. ("Nostrae sibimet opiniones adversantur, ut tibi anima nullam, mihi contra omnes artes secum attulisse se videatur, nec aliud quidquam esse id quod dicitur discere quam reminisci et recordari.")[2]

It is true that we are not always conscious of this knowledge stored in the mind's repository, and we are tempted to believe that it is not there. When we reflect upon the fact, that all that we know must be brought up out of the mind itself, then the function of the mind, by which it is able to do it, assumes a very important aspect. "Recordatio" has a place in it. It does not bring anything and everything into consciousness, but it sifts and distinguishes between those elements which offer themselves for entrance.

The writings of Augustine are full of references to

[1] *Conf.*, x, 21.
[2] *De Quant. Anim.*, xx.

various aspects of the memory. In one passage he treats of the power of the mind over the operations of the memory. "This power of my memory, my God, is great. How great it is!"[1]

His remarks on memory in connection with the subject of sound and especially the human voice, are most interesting. "To understand the sciences, of which we have received no images by the senses, but which we think about in our mind without any image, and wonder what they are in themselves—this, indeed, is nothing else than to arrange, by means of our thought, those notions, which were scattered hither and thither without any order in our memory, and by careful consideration to classify them according to the places where they lay neglected, so that they may be always ready to present themselves with ease to us, when we desire to turn our attention to them."

In *De Mus.*, vi, 6, Augustine speaks of the elusive character of memory, and in *Conf.*, x, 8, he proceeds to classify the contents of memory. He refers to auditory images. He writes, "For while I am dwelling in darkness and in silence, I can call up in my memory, if I choose, colours and distinguish between black and white, and sounds do not rush in and disturb my meditation upon what was drawn in by my eyes, though they too are there, remaining in a separate place." He remembers not merely objectively but as the experience of the self as such. "There also I meet with myself, and I remember myself, what I did, and when, and where, and in what way, when I did it and how I felt."

In another treatise,[2] Augustine states that memory

---

[1] *Conf.*, x, 8.
[2] *De Mag.*, xii, 39.

stores up the images of perception. In the process of perception we receive an impression of the objects, in a way similar to that in which the wax receives the impress of the seal. These images are stored up in the memory; in the chambers of the memory they are carefully arranged as documents of past things and events. ("Ita illas imagines in memoriae penetralibus rerum ante sensarum quaedam documenta gestamus.")

According to Augustine, the higher objects perceived by the mind, as contrasted with the contents of sense perception, which memory serves, are ever present, and there is no past for them.[1] The images of memory are not to be thought of in terms of quantitative measurements, and the fact that memory can hold in itself such immense images is, in Augustine's judgment, a proof of the soul's non-corporeal nature.

He, also, points out that there are two kinds of memory —a memory of that which is the result of the operation of sense, and a memory which is the result of the intellect. The former can recognise everything of a material nature. The recollections which the former kind of memory furnishes are, generally, nothing else than "the images which the spirit has perceived as the result of the impressions which have been made by different bodies upon the organs of the senses. Our power over these images is practically absolute. We can retain within our memory those which we have received, or can share, multiply, rearrange, diffuse, command or distort them."[2]

The latter kind of memory is a purely spiritual phenomenon. Intellectual memory recalls our passions and the different conditions of our spirit. It is a remarkable

[1] *De Mag.*, xii; *De Ord.*, ii, 2.
[2] *De Vera Relig.*, x.

fact that we can recall our passions (without actually experiencing their effects), our sorrows with feelings of joy and our joys with feelings of sadness.

In *Conf.*, ix, 19, we have a remarkable analysis of the process of forgetting, or imperfect recall. An imperfect memory-image, Augustine explains, is a kind of outline which lacks the filling in. When we forget, he points out, we search by means of memory itself, "and there, if one thing be perchance offered instead of another, we reject it, until we meet with that, of which we are in search, and when we have recollected it, we say 'This is it'; it has not entirely vanished into nothingness, but the part that is retained leads us to seek the other, because the memory feels that the whole, to which it is accustomed, is missing." "Maimed of this accustomed part," he adds, "it appears to limp ('claudicans') and presses for the restoration of what was missing." This appears to be a most fitting expression for the experience of an imperfect reminiscence.

In *Conf.*, x, 15, Augustine refers to the difficulty of knowing exactly how emotions and mental states are recalled, but when he asks about these emotions: "Where do I recognise it, but in the memory itself," he is less accurate than usual. It is correct to say that there is an actual exercise of memory in recalling what is meant by "memory," but it is not this present act that is "remembered," but a generalised concept drawn from the numerous cases of the experience of remembering. It would, therefore, be more correct, to say that memory is remembered "by its image" than "by itself." Augustine proceeds as follows: "What, when I name forgetfulness, and withal recognise what I name?" He seems to imply that the same process ought to apply to the remembrance of "oblivio" as to that of "memoria," but in the former the theory that remembrance consists of the complete revival of the experience leads to the paradox that when *we* remember what "oblivio" is we are in a state of oblivion!

A certain carelessness is evident in Augustine's use of the word "oblivio." Augustine then suggests a difficulty which is somewhat artificial, and he asks[1]: "But when it was present, how did it impress its image on the memory, seeing that forgetfulness, by its presence, effaces even what it finds already jotted down?" The condition of being unable to recall something which we wish to recall, is a definite mental experience with distinctive sensory and emotional characteristics which "inscribe themselves on the memory" as clearly as in the case of any other mental state. The confusion arises from Augustine's different employment of the word "oblivio" already referred to.

Augustine gives illustrations of "association by contiguity" in *De Trin.*, xiv, 17, and of "association by similarity" in *De Mus.*, vi, 22. "There occurs to the thought by occasion of similar things, a movement of the mind which is not yet extinct, and this is what is called 'reminiscence'" (recordatio). Illustrations are also given of the "will to remember."

In *De Quant. Anim.*, lxii, Augustine distinguishes with remarkable clearness between the habitual or mechanical memory, arising from repetition, and the intellectual and voluntary memory. "Ascend to the next grade," he writes, "and consider memory, not that which arises from habit of familiar things, but of those innumerable things which are committed to memory by intellectual observation and retained by signs."

Augustine emphasises also the importance of noting

[1] Ch. 16.

the different kinds of memory. He distinguishes the memory of transient things and of those which remain.[1] He even relegates a certain kind of memory to a lower part of the soul.[2]

He speaks of another kind of memory and continues: "I call to mind my father who left me and is now no more: I call to mind Carthage which I left and which still remains." Everything, accordingly, applies to the past and memory has for its object, on the one hand, an object which continues, and, on the other hand, an object which has ceased to exist.[3] It is not only in this narrow and equivocal sense that Augustine recognises a memory of things which do not pass away. This kind of memory, is, in his eyes, reminiscence. He did not, doubtless, accept every kind of reminiscence as true, and he even rejected some of the principles of the Socratic and Platonic doctrine on the subject of reminiscence. He retained and upheld, however, that which is held to be true; he proclaimed the noble doctrine, which Plato and Socrates taught, when they affirmed that knowledge was not so much the acquisition of new ideas as the reminiscence of what is past.

Augustine is not willing to discover, even in his own memory, any idea of God which was the result of his reason. Memory comes into operation sometimes spontaneously, and sometimes under the influence of the Will, which results in concentration. Attention, which regulates the operations of memory, clarifies and regulates them more and more.[4]

---

[1] *Ep.*, vii; *Nebridio*, i.
[2] *De Ord.*, ii, 2.
[3] *Ep.*, vii; *Nebridio*, i.
[4] *Conf.*, xi, 28; *De Trin.*, xi, 7.

The subject of the "will to remember" is also treated of in connection with the law of association in *De Trin.*, xi, 12. Augustine points out that the will to remember cannot arise if the "forgotten" incident is really wholly forgotten. "For example, if I wish to remember what I supped on yesterday, either I have already remembered that I did sup, or if not so, yet at least I have remembered something about supper-time, if nothing else; at all events I have remembered yesterday, and that part of the day in which people usually sup. . . . For if I had remembered nothing at all of this kind I could not remember what I had supped on yesterday."

A very interesting detail in connection with the power of memory is recorded by Augustine: "I can distinguish the odour of lilies and violets when neither is present," i.e. he can by imagination "sense" the difference, as if the smells were present.[1] His powers of sensation were, accordingly, wonderfully keen, and the impression is confirmed by what he tells us about the liveliness of his visualising faculty, e.g. in *De Trin.*, viii, 7, he mentions that when he read the Pauline Epistles all the persons mentioned appeared before his mind's eye. He also mentions that when listening to Church music in which he took a great delight, he was prone to allow the mere aesthetic pleasure to outstrip his devotional feeling.[2] He thus recognises clearly the two tendencies which have always caused the feelings of men to differ in regard to worship—the desire for beautiful and appropriate expression, on the one hand; the fear lest aesthetic feeling should usurp the place of devotion, on the other.

In *Sol.* ii, 20, Augustine refers to the power of

[1] *Conf.*, x.
[2] *Conf.*, x, 33.

recollection as an element in memory, which is termed "recordatio." By means of this, the mind recalls to consciousness what at the moment was not there. Augustine illustrates the efforts to recall a man's name. "If any other name should occur to us and it does not connect itself with him, because we have been accustomed to associate it with him, we therefore reject it, until at last that name comes back to us which fits into its place and completes satisfactorily the usual impression." In the process of recollection, one thing after the other is rejected till at last we find the thing required. This faculty within "recordatio" is "discretio."

The question whether memory involved images of the Phantasia is treated of in the Epistle to Nebridius.[1] Augustine concludes that it does not, because we remember not only past things, but also things which are not past at all. It had been suggested that memory invariably involved Phantasy, which recalled things to mind through images.

A sufficient answer to this question can be found in the reference to the recollection of those eternal verities which have no past and no images. By proving that memory is not exclusively concerned with things in the past, Augustine shows his disregard for those who rejected the Socratic doctrine of Anamnesis.

Thimme[2] considers that the treatment of Memory by Plotinus is superior to that by Augustine. The former rejects the notion of Memory images altogether. Augustine emphasises the fact that these images are not quantitative, but it would have been simpler if he also had formed his theory without them.

[1] *Ep.* vii.
[2] *Augustins geistige Entwickelung,* p. 142.

Imagination

Next above memory in the scale of mental life is placed imagination.

Imagination differs from memory, in that in memory, we believe in the actuality of the remembered thing; in imagination, we do not. Memory yields knowledge of actuality, whereas imagination does not.

It may be pointed out that imagination is stronger than a mere wish. If there is a wish on the one hand and imagination on the other, the imagination result is more likely to occur than the wish result; indeed, the situation is one of frustrated will. The process of wishing approximates to volition or will, but it has not yet reached the complete state of volition. In the transition from wishing to willing, to volition, the imagination, illumined and intensified by fear or some other disturbing emotion, slips in, as it were, takes the lead, and prevents the wish becoming the will. Imagination then wins because the will has not been completed.[1]

The Letter to Nebridius[2] furnishes us with Augustine's most important teaching on this subject. Nebridius had argued that imagination can create its own materials independently of the senses and that it is possible to imagine things that have never been seen.

Augustine replies: "Whence comes, you ask, our capacity for conceiving in thought things which we have never seen? Whence do you think, save from a certain faculty or subtracting or adding which is innate in the mind?" In another treatise he gives examples of an imaginary bird completely unknown to him, such as a black swan, or a four-legged bird. He adds:" Therefore

[1] See *Hibbert Journal*, April, 1925, p. 405.
[2] *Ep.*, vii.

it is possible for the mind to produce by the exercise of the imagination that which as a whole has never been experienced by the senses, but the parts have all been present to the senses in a variety of different connections."

In some restricted manner, imagination is dependent on memory. In effect, if memory can operate without imagination, the exercise of the imagination, on the contrary, presupposes that of memory. In the psychology of Augustine, therefore, imagination is not reduced to a mere imaginative faculty. Certain materials are necessary to enable the imagination to operate; these it even transforms and modifies. The presence of these materials, which furnish it with sense and reason in turn, is due to memory.[1]

Phantasia

There is but little concerning Phantasia in the earlier writings of Augustine. He is conscious of the fact that it is a foreign name and it is not fully naturalised in his vocabulary; consequently, he sometimes uses the Latin term "imaginatio" as an alternative. Augustine is inclined, on the one hand, to regard "imaginatio" as an illegitimate element in the soul, a disturber of the pure vision of Ratio; for "imaginatio" draws its images from the perceptions, and introduces them into the holy of holies of the mind, where they are liable to cause confusion with the real ideas, the only true source of the highest knowledge; these false images are the "imaginations" ("magna cautione vitandae"[2]).

Imaginatio is a creative faculty, but it cannot soar as high as Ratio. By its means, we call up images in the mind.[3]

[1] *Ep.*, vii, *to Nebridius*, i.
[2] *Solil.*, ii, 20.
[3] *Solil.*, ii, 20.

With regard to its creative, image-forming character, it is also called "cogitatio imaginaria." There is a limit, beyond which its creative power cannot go. Having, for instance, formed the mental picture of two lines in a circle, between which not even the finest point could be placed, Imaginatio declares it can introduce no more lines between, but Ratio cries out immediately that innumerable lines can be drawn there.

In classifying Phantasia, or imaginatio, we may regard it as a part of the Memory of Perceptions, though not of the Memory associated with Anamnesis.

In *Conf.*, x, 35, Augustine gives an example of the remarkable vividness with which he can reconstruct a psychological situation. He imagines the spectator of a horror gloating over it even while he remarks that he fears it will disturb his dreams.

He, also, leads up to the introduction of a refinement of terminology by distinguishing two kinds of imaginary images. One of these is that of ordinary pictorial imaginations such as the image that we form, in reading the poets, of the appearance of Aeneas, or of Medea and her winged dragons. The other kind is that of schematic images that we make in order to assist our thought, such as geometrical figures and figures to represent the world. He further explains that whereas Nebridius classified all three kinds—the memory image, the pictorial imagination, and the schematic image—together as "phantasiae," he himself purposed to reserve "phantasia" for the simple memory image, the mental image produced by actual sense impression, and to designate the imaginary constructions as "phantasmata," the visual image formed by arbitrarily combining and working up sense impressions.[1]

1 *De Mus.*, vi, 32.

The memory image of his father he describes as a "phantasma." Augustine appears to have been the first Latin writer to use the words in a philosophical sense.

Augustine, however, does not confine the operation of imagination to the world of sense. He recognises, also, an intellectual imagination, which can operate upon the principles furnished by reason. "Omnes has imagines . . . in tria genera commodissime ac verissime distribui video: Quorum est unum sensis rebus impressum, alterum putatis, alterum ratis."[1] Augustine not only refused to restrict imagination to the imaginative faculty, but exalted it above phantasy, that is to say, the imaginative faculty which combines and recognises it, in certain cases, as an object purely intellectual.

He has good reasons for continually exhorting us to lull to rest the shadows and the phantoms of the imagination and the desire to suppress the activities of this dangerous faculty. "Nullo enim modo resistitur corporis sensibus, quae nobis sacratissima disciplina est, si per eos inflictus plagis vulneribusque blandimur."[2]

Hallucination, Mental Aberration and Mystery of Dreams

Augustine has various references to, and illustrations of, these mental activities. He says that intense concentration may give rise to hallucination.[3] His observations on delirium are set forth in De Gen. ad Litt., xii, 25. An account of second-sight is given in De Gen. ad Litt., xii, 35. He also describes a remarkable dream which he had.[4]

---

[1] Epis. vii; Nebridio, ii.
[2] Id. Ch. iii.
[3] De Trin., xi, 7.
[4] De Gen. ad Litt., xii, 3.

Psycho-Physical Phenomena

In St. Augustine's accounts of his mystical experiences there does not appear to be any suggestion of ecstasy, trance, or quasi-hypnotic phenomena, yet the essentials of ecstasy were familiar to him. In *De Gen. ad Litt.*, xii, where he refers to St. Paul's description of his mysterious experience,[1] he treats of problems involved in these phenomena. In the same book he also describes the physical aspect of ecstasy. "It is a state midway between sleep and death. The soul is rapt (rapitur) in such a manner as to be withdrawn (overtatur) from the bodily senses more than in sleep, but less than in death."[2] And again in xii, 12, he writes, "When the attention of the mind is wholly turned away and withdrawn (penitus avertitur atque abripitur) from the bodily senses, it is called ecstasy. Then whatever bodies may be present are not seen with the open eyes, nor is any voice heard at all."

Accordingly, ecstasy is a departure ("excessus") of the mind which sometimes happens through fright, but sometimes as the result of some revelation; it takes place by means of an alienation of the mind from the senses of the body, in order that to the spirit may be shown what is to be revealed.[3] In *Enar.* ii, in *Ps.* xxx, Serm. 1, 2. it is stated that ecstasy is caused by fright or by rapt attention ("intentia") to things above, in such a way that earthly things no longer have a place in the memory.

St. Augustine's ideas on the subject of the psychology of ecstasy are also referred to in *De Gen. ad Litt.*, xii, 5, with reference to St. Paul's words in II Cor., xii, 3: "He did not know whether, when rapt to the third heaven,

---

[1] 2 Cor., xii, 2–4.

[2] *De Gen. ad Litt.*, xii, 26.

[3] *Enar., Ps.*, lxvii, 36.

he was in the body, as the soul is in the body when the body is said to live, be it of one awake or of one asleep, or when in ecstasy the soul is alienated from the bodily senses; or whether his soul had altogether gone forth from his body, so that the body lay dead, until, when the revelation was over, his soul was restored to the dead members: so that he did not awake as one asleep, nor, as one alienated in ecstasy, and return to his senses; but as one dead came to life again. But because, when his soul was alienated from his body, it was uncertain whether it left his body quite dead, or after some manner of a living body the soul was there, but his mind was carried away to see or hear the unspeakable things of that vision—for this reason, perhaps, he said: 'Whether in the body or out of the body, I know not; God knoweth.' "

In *Liber de Videndo Dei*[1] a distinction is drawn between the soul (anima) which during an ecstasy remains in the body, and the mind (mens) which is withdrawn from the bodily senses. Here Augustine strives with the greatest precision to attain to scientific accuracy and, for this reason, the passage is the one most in harmony with the data of psychology.

The Subconscious and Memory

Many memory traces are readily accessible and easily enter the stream of consciousness as the result of appropriate stimulus. Other memory traces, on the other hand, are not readily accessible. They lie, as it were, deeper in the structure of the mind, and are brought into consciousness only when the stimulus is specially strong or with the aid of conscious effort. Others again are not accessible at all under normal conditions, but are aroused

[1] *Ep.*, 147.

only under special conditions or by special methods. It is the existence of this last class which led Professor Freud to develop his theory of the unconscious. All memory traces comprised in the first two classes may be said to lie in the region of the foreconscious, i.e. there is no special barrier to prevent their coming into consciousness. In the case of the last class, however, there exist special repressive barriers which have to be broken down before the memory traces can come into consciousness.[1]

The Subconscious

The conception of the subconscious or the unconscious probably originated with Leibniz, who termed it "petites perceptions," and may be said to have been introduced into psychology from philosophy. Myers[2] points out that the conscious self of each of us is only a small part of the real self: that underneath the conscious personality there exists a much larger "sub-liminal" self, below the threshold of our immediate awareness, dominating many of our actions and our thoughts by powers not known to us, and constituting the real and essential personality, of which the conscious self is but a broken gleam. Psychic elements may thus rise from the subconscious into the stream of consciousness. The one true self is the totality of consciousness of which the supraliminal part is a fraction. Myers is supported in his theory to a great degree by William James, whereas other writers describe sub-consciousness as the fringe or background of the mind. Another meaning sometimes assigned to the term "subconscious" makes it identical with the unconscious and interprets the

[1] See Tansley. *The New Psychology*, p. 50.
[2] *Human Personality*, vol. I, p. 12.

unconscious in terms of physiological processes. The unconscious is also the storehouse of racial memory and of repressed experience.

Modern psychology pays great attention to sub-conscious powers of the mind, yet no one has explained them better than Augustine in *Conf.*, x, where he speaks of memory as the mysterious storehouse of a vast collection of forgotten knowledge and impressions. Not only is apparently forgotten knowledge there, but also powers, instincts, intuitions, both good and bad, highest and lowest; they are all at work in this hidden region, and only now and then, they arise above the threshold of consciousness. Many psychologists consider that mystical states are part of the contents of the subconscious region, and are really latent powers which emerge from sub-consciousness into consciousness—"inroads from the subconscious life, of the cerebral activity correlative to which we as yet know nothing."[1]

The seat of the faculties of the soul, of intellection and understandings of reason, will, emotion and imagination, is the soul itself; the spiritual principle is the root of all the faculties. This view will certainly be held by all who believe the mind to be something more than a bundle of sensations, phantasmata, emotions, cognitions and volitions.

Augustine approaches very nearly to the modern conception of the subconscious mind in *De Trin.*, xv, 40. He has been speaking on the subject of memory in the ordinary sense, and then he goes on to say: "But there is a lower depth (abstrusior profunditas) of our memory in which we discovered that truth, when we began to think about it."

We must remember that any sharp division between "will" and "nature" is unsound psychology. The self is

[1] W. James. *Varieties*, p. 427.

always a great deal more than the content of consciousness at any given moment. The conscious and the unconscious shade off into one another. There are, probably, very few conscious acts in most men's lives which express at all fully the character of the doer. But dispositions, as well as acts, have moral quality, and all that lies below the threshold will form part of a final moral estimate of the man.

The will never decides without a motive, without the attraction of some good which it perceives in the object. Now, although the will may be free in the presence of every motive, still, as a matter of fact, it forms different resolutions according to the various motives presented to it. The orator can do no more than suggest motives. What a power over the will a man would enjoy, who could, at his own pleasure, at any moment, and in the most striking manner, present this or any other motive of action! But such is God's privilege.

We may also add, with Augustine, that not only does God suggest at His pleasure those attractive motives which inspire the will with its determinations, but, before choosing between these illuminations of the natural and the supernatural order, God knows the response which the soul, with all freedom, will make to each of them. Therefore, in the Divine Knowledge, there is for each created will an indefinite series of motives which de facto (but very freely) win man's consent to what is good.

Dreams

Dream life occupies a specially important place in modern psychology, because it can be shown that in dreams the mind is freed from some of the limitations which restrict its operation during waking life. Dreams, consequently, enable us to supplement our knowledge of the mind which is derived solely from the waking life; they throw much light on the by-ways of the libido, and give us a much more complete picture of the contents of the mind as a whole. Certain functions of the mind, such as symbolization, the activity of which is restricted in the waking life of the ordinary individual, have, for instance, much freer play in dreams, while in dream life the repressions of waking life are in a certain sense, though by no means wholly, removed.

Mr. Tansley[1] mentions that certain definite and indisputable characteristics of dream life have long been well-known. Prominent among these is dream memory, which has the power of recalling pictures and events that have long dropped out of the waking memory. Another feature is that some of the material of every dream is based on quite recent experience, usually that of the preceding day. A third is the fact that external sense impressions during sleep often actually initiate dreams.

By studying the working of the dreaming mind important insight is given, both into mental content and into mental processes. They throw light on the unconscious and half-conscious contents of the mind because they are able to express, owing to release from the consciousness inhibition of the waking state, what cannot be expressed in waking life.

Augustine, in *De Gen. ad Litt.*, xii, 3, describes a curious dream, the details of which he appears to have accurately remembered and which contains a certain psychological interest: "But it has sometimes happened to me, and I do not doubt, therefore, that it may have happened to others, that when seeing things in a dream I have

[1] *The New Psychology*, p. 132.

known that I was seeing them in a dream, and although asleep have been firmly convinced that those images which usually delude us into accepting them are not real corporeal objects. But on some such occasions I have been so far deceived that I tried to convince a friend of mine, whom I also saw in the dream, that the things which we saw were not real objects, but dream images, though I certainly saw him just in the same way as I saw them. I told him also that it was not even true that we were talking together, but that he himself was seeing something else in a dream and was quite unaware that I was seeing those things. But at the same time that I was trying to persuade him that he was not real, I was partly inclined to think him real, for I should certainly not have spoken to him if I had altogether believed him to be unreal."

The Rational Faculties

Speaking of the rational faculties it may be mentioned that the term "animus" is always used by Augustine of the soul in its higher relations and functions, whereas "anima" is assigned a wider meaning, although it often apparently has the same meaning as "animus."[1]

"Ratio" is the organ of the highest faculty, although at times there appears to be some uncertainty as to its real meaning.[2]

Ratio or mens is the best part of man, which the whole man has to respect and obey.[3] Ratio claims obedience in man's "mikrokosmos" and is the principle of order both in the universe and in the individual life. Upon it is founded the eternal law, for Ratio is itself eternal,

[1] Cf. De Beat. Vit., ii, 8; De Ord., ii, 3.
[2] Cf. De Lib. Arb., i, 8; De Immort. Anim., ii; Solil., i, 1.
[3] Cont. Acad., i, 2.

unchangeable, and therefore to be always implicitly obeyed.[1]

Ratio is that endowment of man which exalts him above all the world around him, even above invisible powers mysterious and ineffable, dwelling we know not where.[2] Man, however, is liable to treat this valuable gift with too little care; as the result of too much haste and too little deliberation we run the risk of losing confidence in the trustworthiness even of Plato.[3]

The *Soliloquies* are cast into the form of a dialogue between Reason and Self. But, however dominant the part of Reason may be, Augustine is convinced that Reason alone is not competent to determine spiritual qualities. Augustine subjects himself to a severe self-examination concerning his motives. He is now thirty-three years of age. He asks himself whether his mind is set on *money-making*. He believes that for the last fourteen years he has not been ambitious in this respect. Cicero's book *Hortensius* taught him that wealth should not be an object of pursuit, but that if it was acquired, it should be administered with the highest caution and prudence. Augustine feels that all his ambition in this respect is to have sufficient for his maintenance.

He next examines himself about *ambition*. He realises that until quite recently he was dominated by a longing to acquire honours and distinctions. There is a glamour about worldly success which fascinated him. He feels, however, that this stage has now passed.

He then asks himself about *marriage*. He replies that for himself he neither seeks nor desires it. He adds the

[1] *De Lib. Arb.*, i, 6.
[2] *Cont. Acad.*, i, 7.
[3] *De Magist.*, x, 31.

following comment on his view of the duties of the married. Whether the procreation of children was part of the function of the wise, which at present he was not able to say, we might concede that any person who entered the married state for this purpose only was to be admired but not imitated. For its dangers were more evident than its blessedness. Evidently Augustine was feeling humiliated by his inconsistencies.

In this merciless self-analysis he owns himself greatly disturbed by three chief apprehensions—the fear of loss, the fear of death, and the fear of pain.

Augustine defines Ratio and Ratiocinatio in terms similar to Plotinus.[1] Woerter[2] is inclined to think that Augustine borrowed this definition from Plotinus.

Ratio in *De Quant. Anim.* is defined as that inseparable, essential, and characteristic function of the mind, by means of which it is capable of attaining knowledge.

Ratiocinatio is the process itself, in which the mind is actually engaged when searching for knowledge. The wise man is not always engaged in the search for wisdom, but he is never without the power to search and to find Ratio.[3] Ratio is the mind's power of vision, so to speak ("Ratio quidam mentis aspectus") and Ratiocinatio implies the sweep of the horizon in the eye's search for an object. Ratio is thus, potentially, Ratiocinatio or "ratiocinandi potestas."

We see the Ratiocinatio at work in comparing and judging, whereas Ratio is apparent in the principles by which it judges. He suggests that the intuitive reason is at work in supplying data for the laws of thought, the

[1] Plotinus. *Ennead* III, 8, ch. 11.
[2] P. 45.
[3] *De Quant. Anim.*, xxvii, 52.

laws of mathematics, and the sense of harmony which makes us admire beauty in art and nature.

Knowledge is vision, and ignorance is a lack of it ("cum autem non videt mens quamvis intendit aspectum, inscitia vel ignorantia dicitur"). The mind directs its gaze, but that gaze results in no vision, for the mind itself is in darkness.

Augustine is influenced to formulate a further definition of knowledge. To know is to live with a greater sense of reality and a greater intelligence.[1] Knowledge is thus vision and life.

We can recognise the influence of Platonism on the mind of Augustine, when he describes Ratio as the eye of the soul, and Scientia as vision. For Plato, the source of all Being, and of Truth, and of knowledge is the Good.

In various ways Augustine emphasises the importance of the direct, immediate character of knowledge. Because our ideas are innate, all learning is Anamnesis or Recollection. Consequently, all instruction implies previous knowledge; and words, in themselves, are signs and not the means of fresh illumination; they do not teach ("discere"). Concerning Perception, our knowledge of nature is intuitive. He seems to imply that we possess already the ideas of the objects which we see, and thus immediately recognise them. Immediate observation suffices to acquire a knowledge of nature. Man recognises the meaning of sun, and moon, and stars, instinctively.[2]

Not only nature, but everything else is known immediately. The name of a thing is meaningless to us until we have seen the thing itself; the name then becomes a sign. If this be so, however, is it ever possible to know

[1] De Lib. Arb., i, 7, 17.
[2] De Magis., x, 32.

the facts of history? We cannot come into contact with those facts, we have only the words in which the history is set forth.

The story of the three men in the fiery furnace in Babylon furnishes a suitable illustration. Furnace, fire, king and the other elements are terms known to us, but the men themselves are stranger to us, and the names in themselves tell us nothing. Clearly faith must precede knowledge, and in fact displace it.[1]

In *De Quant. Anim.*, xiii, we have an exposition of the principle that like is known through like. One of Augustine's chief proofs of the incorporeal nature of the soul is that it can recognise the incorporeal. Body, for the simple reason that it is so unlike the objects of higher knowledge, can never attain to this knowledge.

The Disciplinae

Augustine uses the term Disciplina to signify a special Science. The subject matter of the Disciplinae vary, but knowledge remains the same in them all.[2]

On the other hand, a discipline, although always representing a systematised body of knowledge, is often clearly conceived of, not as lying outside the mind, but within it. It implies, moreover, conscious knowledge and, therefore, can be said to be only in the mind of one who is learning, by which is meant a person who has already learnt something.[3]

The Disciplinae have the source of their intelligibility in God. Just as God Himself is intelligible, so are the contents of the Disciplinae likewise intelligible, but these

[1] *De Magis.*, xi, 37.
[2] *Solil.* I, iv, 10.
[3] *De Immort. Anim.*, i; *Cont. Acad.*, iii, 3.

latter are intelligible in the light of the divine reason shed upon them. The earth would not be visible were it not illumined by the light of the sun. Therefore, the contents of the Disciplinae are undoubtedly true, but their truth is rooted outside of themselves in God. He is the Sun, Himself visible, by Whose light they are illumined.[1]

True knowledge aims everywhere at the discovery of Truth, but there are different stages of knowledge, according to the object in which Truth is present. These stages show the continuity of all knowledge, from that of the humblest object to the knowledge of God. In the final stage the beholder gazes upon Veritas itself. The Disciplinae, accordingly, form an ascending series, for they train and lead the mind upwards.[2]

The Disciplinae embrace the ordinary spheres of art and culture. Music is included in the Disciplinae, but by reason of its double-sided nature, contemplating ideas on the one hand, and sounds on the other, it partakes both of the senses and of the intellect.[3]

The highest of the Disciplinae is the Science of Dialectics, and it provides us with the ground of absolute certainty in the realm of knowledge. No false knowledge is possible here.[4]

This Disciplina is a touchstone of truth. Through dialectics we are assured that whatever is the state of our bodily senses, these things are true. By this science, we know also that logical processes give true results.[5]

---

[1] *Solil.*, i, 8.
[2] Parry. *Augustine and Platonism*, p 79.
[3] *De Ord.*, ii, 14, 41.
[4] *Cont. Acad.*, iii, 13.
[5] *Cont. Acad.*, iii, 13.

CHAPTER VIII

EXISTENCE OF GOD

ST. AUGUSTINE was not of a pre-eminently metaphysical turn of mind. His mind did not work with ease or by preference in the region of abstract ideas and non-material conceptions.

Previous to his Conversion, Augustine, doubtless, experienced some difficulty in evolving the conception of the spiritual nature of God. Under the influence of Mani, he regarded God as a corporate Being,and sought to apply to Him the Aristotelian categories, thus debarring himself from a true knowledge of the Divine nature. His Manichaean principles taught him that Deity could not become incarnate without contamination by contact with a substance which was evil. The Incarnation, therefore, was to him incredible. Accordingly, he recoiled from incredibilities which he ascribed to the Catholic religion, but which were, in reality, the product of his own misconceptions.

Augustine refers to this mental attitude in at least three passages of the *Confessions*: "Seeing that I knew no way of thinking of God save as a corporal Being—for it did not seem to me possible for anything to exist except in this form—that was the greatest and almost the sole cause of the error which held me fast."[1] "What is meant by a spiritual substance I could not form even a faint and shadowy notion";[2] "So slow of heart was I . . . that whatsoever was not extended in space, I supposed to have no existence at all."[3]

Majestic Platonian speculation helped to exalt him at

[1] v, 19. [2] vi, 4. [3] vii, 2.

last to a higher conception of God ... of God viewed as a unit, as a pure spirit, as infinite perfection. The discipline of that highly abstract philosophy greatly strengthened this aspect of his thought. He also informs us that the sermons of Ambrose and Theodorus delivered him for the first time from the prejudice that the Catholic Church taught that the Deity was fashioned like man, and he came to think of God and of the Soul as incorporeal.[1]

Some Fathers, especially those influenced by Aristotle, declared the knowledge of God, in its whole extent, to be innate (e.g. Arnobius)—a knowledge to be constantly tested by the observation of nature. No difficulty is raised by reason of the fact that some of the Fathers described the existence of God and His distinctive nature as capable of proof; others, as incapable; for the latter rejected the proof only in so far as God could not be discovered by means of deduction "a prius." "The psychological, cosmological, and natural theological proofs were not despised by them," Harnack observes, when controverting the teaching of Atheism, Polytheism, Manichaeism, etc.

We find in St. Augustine's writings certain suggestions of an ontological proof. His line of argument was directed first to demonstrate rules of human thought, which accordingly transcended it. Augustine maintains that these rules are *truths*, and that their sum is the *truth*. This truth is a living power, therefore it exists. Thus the way to prove the existence of God is opened.

The Neo-Platonists recognised that God was inscrutable. They asserted that "whatever the creature is, that God is not"[2]. "Even if it is not possible to comprehend

[1] *Conf.*, v; *De Beata. Vita*, i, 4.
[2] *Athan. ad Monach.*, 2.

what God is, it is possible to say what He is not." The
Fathers, influenced by Neo-Platonism, however, assumed
that the contemplative ascetic, who was on the way to
deification, could gain a direct vision of God in all His
splendour. Augustine describes[1] the impossibility of
declaring the nature of God—a statement that coincides
exactly with the tenets of the Basilidians.[2]

The subject of the existence of God is treated of by
Augustine in the *Soliloquies*, in *De Libero Arbitrio*, and in
other treatises. It may be stated that all of the classic
proofs of God's existence may be found in the Works of
Augustine, though seldom in logical form.

(1) There is the proof of God's existence *from universal
consent*. Augustine believed that no rational creature "so
long as it makes use of its reason" can be entirely ignorant
of God. "With the exception of a few in whom nature has
become outrageously depraved," he writes, "the whole
race of man acknowledges God as the Maker of this
World."[3] With everyone in full possession of his faculties
admitting the existence of God, it is evident that logical
proofs are purely gratuitous.

If any should say that they deny God's existence
Augustine asks, "Why should I consider the method of
dealing with them, when it is doubtful whether they
ought to be dealt with at all?" He adds that he addresses
himself ordinarily not to depraved but to normal men,
"who do not deny the existence of God, and who,
moreover, allow that human affairs are not disregarded by
Him."[4]

[1] *De Doct. Chr.*, i, 6.
[2] *Hippol. Philos.*, vii, 20.
[3] In *Joan. Evang. Tr.*, CVI, xvii, 4.
[4] *De Mor. Eccl. Cath.*, vi, 10.

In *Enarratio in Psalmum*, xiii, 2, Augustine shows that no man who makes use of his reason denies that there is a God. It is only the depraved man, the fool who says it, and he dares to say it only in his heart. The fool alone says it and his folly is due to the degradation of his soul. Only a few, however, are discovered of such great impiety; "rare is the man who says in his heart, 'There is no God.'"

(2) Augustine gives us also *the testimony of the Bible* to the existence of God. Not only have we the testimony of the writer of Genesis who recorded "In the beginning God created the heavens and the earth," a fact revealed to the writer, Augustine affirms, by God Himself, but we have the further written testimony of many men who say that they lived with the Son of God and saw miracles performed "which could never have been done if there were no God."[1] We have also the evidence of the fulfilment of many of the Old Testament prophecies which testifies to the existence of the Divine Being who inspired those prophets and thus guarantees that He is the one true God.[2]

(3) Apart from the appeal to authority, Augustine endeavours to prove that God's existence may also be known *by reason*. In *De Lib. Arbit.*, Augustine says that faith must precede proof: "Nor does anyone become fit to discover God, unless he shall have first believed what he is later to know."[3] He further states that while we ought to accept in faith God's existence, we may also come to a sure, although incomplete knowledge of Him through reason.[4] The fact that the pagan philosophers believed

---

[1] *De Lib. Arb.*, II, ii 5.
[2] *De Serm. Domini in Monte*, I, xix 27.
[3] *De Lib. Arbit.*, ii, 2.
[4] *Ibid.*

in the existence of God is an evidence that it may be known by reason outside of all revelation and all faith. This also indicates that there is no conflict between reason and faith. On the other hand, the shortest and surest road to a knowledge of God is by faith and not by reason.

(4) Augustine believes that the *ontological proof* is a demonstration of God's existence from the very idea of God and is consequently a proof by reason alone. It produces conviction, however, only in the mind of him who already holds by faith what the demonstration attempts to prove by reason.

It may be mentioned that much of Anselm's ontological argument in the *Proslogion* may be found in Augustine's teaching. Both writers believe that faith should precede reason; both identify the supreme good and most real being; both are justified by their realism in proceeding from thought to existence. The proof both of Anselm and of Augustine involves the whole metaphysical system.

(5) Another proof of the existence of God produced by Augustine is that of the *witness of the inner reason or soul*. If we would know that God exists we need only turn within ourselves, looking away from the things of sense and letting God lead us until, with the eye of our souls, above our minds we see the Unchangeable Light. In the contemplation of Truth, also, one discovers God. "For where I found Truth," says Augustine, "there found I my God, the Truth itself; which since I learned, I have not forgotten."[1] In the contemplation of Truth God seems to speak and the heart hears Him.[2] So sure is

---

[1] *Conf.*, x, 24.
[2] *Conf.*, vii, 10.

this witness of the heart that one who has once beheld and heard it can never again doubt the existence of God or Truth. Augustine adds: "It is easier to doubt that I live than that Truth is not."

(6) A further proof is furnished *by a study of the "creature."* The created character of the world implies a creator. As we scrutinise the various works of God, Augustine tells us, "we may detect, as it were, His footprints, now more now less distinct even in those things that are beneath us." "They could not so much as exist," he continues, " or be bodied forth in any shape, or follow or observe any law, had they not been made by the hand of the most essential, wise and good God."[1] All nature proclaims the fact that it did not make itself. The heavens declare "We are not God, but He made us."[2] The proof of God's existence thus moves by steps from the contemplation of that which changes to the forms which endure, and thence to their immutable source. God is immutable. He is goodness and truth and all perfection. He is the Creator, Upholder and Provider.

The order in the universe thus furnishes evidence of the work of God. All changes and movements in the world are well-ordered, reflecting a purpose and a plan.[3] The soul of an animal regulating its whole body and the members executing their respective functions illustrate this order. Again, the government of the world is a veritable miracle of order and purpose.[4] Measure, form and order demand a supreme measure, a supreme form and a supreme order and must be regarded as generic

[1] *De Civ. Dei*, xi, 28.
[2] *Conf.*, x, 6.
[3] *De Civ. Dei*, xi, 4.
[4] *Cont. Acad.*, i, 1.

goods in things made by God. God must, however, be conceived as above every measure of the creature, above every form, above every order, above not in space but by "ineffable and singular potency."[1]

(7) *The fact of beauty* is another testimony of God's existence. The perception of beauty led Augustine to analyse the faculty which perceives it. In doing so, he is led upward from sensible objects to the sentient soul; thence to the reasoning faculty and, at length, to the eternal, immutable light, which enables reason to form its judgments; to that, indeed, which is the vita vitae—the life of the soul's life.[2]

How the contemplation of these objects of sense led him to contemplate the soul's creator appears in the words: "O beauty, so ancient and so new, behold Thou wast within and I without; and without I sought Thee; and I, deformed as I was, ran after those forms of beauty which Thou hast made. . . . Those things held me back from Thee, which could have no existence save in Thee."[3] In this respect we see a resemblance to the experience of Plotinus.

In *De Lib. Arbit.*, ii, 3, Augustine proceeds to analyse the intellectual process, distinguishing an interior sense from the five senses and the work of reason from that of the interior sense. He then advances his argument as follows: What measures and judges is higher than that which is measured. Truth is found and not made. For example, it is a simple mathematical truth that seven and three make ten. (Augustine had a natural love for numbers.) It is an affirmation of an eternal truth. The

[1] *De Nat. Bon.*, iii.
[2] *Conf.*, x, 6.
    Conf., x, 27.

individual thinker does not cause this to be true. It is true independently of himself. The principle controls his intellect and his will. There is something, therefore, more sublime than our reason. If then there is truth and it is immutable and eternal, this is God or something belonging to a being who must be God. Our freedom consists in subjection to the truth, We are thus compelled to recognise the existence of an unchanging, rational, and moral order above ourselves, which logically and morally constrains us. This order cannot be a mere abstract concept but we must recognise the existence of an eternal Intellect and an eternal Will.

Thus the knowledge of numbers is also a knowledge of God. By distinguishing and connecting these eternal numbers man enters the presence of the immutable and divine. Through them he knows how to attain the happy life and enjoy "the highest measure who is the father of order," guided no longer by faith alone but now also by certain reasons.[1]

It may be pointed out that the Augustinian proof of the existence of God will be found also in the writings of Thomas Aquinas's *Quarta via*. Like Descartes, Augustine derived his proof of the existence of God from the evidence of thought.

The conception that God is the fountain of life to all His creatures led Augustine to lay stress on the truth of the divine immanence. If the soul of man in thought, imagination, and memory is able to contemplate the whole of space, much more must omnipresence be a characteristic of the Creator of the soul.

Eucken says: "To Augustine, God is not a particular somewhat—existing along with things, but the inclusive

[1] *De Ordine*, ii, 19.

totality of true being, beyond which is no reality; to separate oneself from Him means to fall into nothingness: to unite oneself to Him means to rise from appearance to reality."[1]

In his *Confessions*,[2] Augustine has a remarkable phrase about the existence of God. "God is one, Whose being and Whose life are one and the same thing." This thought finds further expression in an important passage in *Joan. Tract.*, 39, 8: "God is that which is": "Ego sum qui sum"; God, therefore, is unchangeable, whereas the soul is changeable. When the soul receives from God the power to be good, it becomes so by participation, as the eye sees by participation (of the light). In the same way, if the soul is good, that goodness, whereof it partakes, is in God whereof, if the soul partakes not, every man is a liar. God is true to His word not by participating in truth, but by begetting it.

The thesis of St. Augustine on the simultaneous creation of the Universe, and the gradual development of the world under the action of the natural forces which were placed in it, suggests to the mind many remarkable thoughts. Certainly, the instantaneous act of the Creator did not produce an organised universe as we see it now. But, in the beginning, God created all the elements of the world in a confused and "nebulous" mass (the words of Augustine are: "nebulosa species apparet"),[3] and in this mass were the mysterious germs ("rationes seminales") of future beings which were to develop themselves, when favourable circumstances should permit. Can we truthfully assert that Augustine was an

---

[1] *The Problem of Human Life*, p. 218.
[2] i, 6.
[3] *De Gen. ad Litt.*, i, 27.

Evolutionist? If we mean that Augustine had a deeper and wider mental outlook than other thinkers had of the forces of nature and the plasticity of beings, this statement is an incontestable fact. Regarded from this point of view, Zahn[1] is right when he felicitates him as the precursor of modern thought. But, on the other hand, if we mean that he recognised in matter a power of differentiation and of gradual transformation, developing from the heterogeneous, the most formal statements, certainly, compel us to recognise that Augustine proclaimed the fixity of species, and did not admit that "from one identical primitive principle, or from one germ, different realities can issue." This judgment of Martin, in his very searching investigation of this subject[2] corrects the conclusion of Zahn. "The elements of this corporeal world have also their well-defined force and their proper quality, on which depends what each one of them can or cannot do, and what reality ought or ought not to issue from each one of them. Hence it is that from a grain of wheat a bean cannot issue, nor wheat from a bean, nor a man from a beast, nor a beast from a man."[3]

God is Triune and, in order to explain His triune personality as well as His Substantial unity, Augustine uses some remarkable psychological illustrations. In *De Trin.*, viii, 14, he mentions a striking analogy of the nature of love. He says that there are three elements in love: "he that loves, that which is loved, and love." Love, he affirms, is that which unites the lover and the beloved. This illustration Augustine recognises as the

[1] *Bible, Science, and Faith*, pp. 58–66.
[2] *S. Augustin*, p. 314.
[3] *De Gen. ad Litt.*, ix, 32.

clearest revelation of the doctrine of the Holy Trinity.
For the most profound of all attributes that can be
believed of the Deity is that "God is Love." Dr. Rashdall
criticised this analysis[1]: "Nobody can possibly think of
the love of one spiritual being for another as a Person in
the modern sense of the term." In fact, Rashdall criticises
St. Augustine's treatise on the Holy Trinity as a whole as
"full of obscurities, inconsistencies, and unintelligi-
bilities."[2]

With regard to the former criticism, Rashdall suggests
that, since love is impersonal, Augustine implies that the
Holy Spirit is impersonal. Even if this appears to be so,
Augustine ascribes a personal relation of mutual love to
the Father and the Son. Even if the analysis is not perfect
Augustine is concerned with love as known among
human beings, and he suggests that Divine love transcends in nature human love. He adds: "It remains for us
to ascend from earth, and to seek those things which are
above, as far as it is possible to man." He adds that in the
Deity is the Lover, the beloved, and the Love which
unites them. This is a relation of mutual intelligence,
which may be described as friendship. Love, therefore,
is not a mere abstraction, but an intelligent Being. He
gives further proof of this in such phrases as: "in Trinity
of Persons mutually inter-related, and a unity of equal
essence,"[3] and he describes the Holy Spirit as a mutual
love, wherewith the Father and the Son reciprocally
love one another."[4] It appears, therefore, that Augustine
applies the same term to the Holy Spirit, and in the same

[1] *Ideas and Ideals*, p. 175.

[2] P. 176.

[3] ix, 1.

[4] xv, 50.

sense in which it is applied to the Father and to the Son.

With regard to the charge of inconsistency it must be borne in mind that Augustine, in this treatise, is endeavouring to do two things, viz. to expound the traditional doctrine of the Church, and to reason concerning the problem of the doctrine, as far as his intellectual power permitted. The operations of faith and reason, accordingly, are considered, but tradition and speculative elements influence the mind of Augustine all through. With regard to the latter, he is, without doubt, still influenced unconsciously by his Neo-Platonist antecedents. "His wonderfully profound analysis of love and of the doctrine that God is love is the clearest proof of his identity with the traditional conception of the Trinity as Unity."[1]

In *De Trin.*, xiv, 12, 15, Augustine sets forth another analogy—the relationship of the mind to God, viz. the operation of memory, intelligence, and love. "Haec igitur trinitas mentis non propterea Dei est imago, quia sui meminet mens, et intellegit ac diligit se; sed quia potest etiam meminisse, et intellegere, et amare a quo facta est."

Suggestions of the Trinity can also be discerned in created things. It is observed, for instance, that everything has a number, a weight, and a measure and yet remains one despite these distinctions.[2]

In *Serm.*, lii, 19–23, and *De Trin.*, xii, Augustine illustrates the Trinity by Memory, Intelligence, and Will. He appears to realise a weakness in his analogy, for he points out that it is only in certain ways that these three suggest an analogy and he explains that these three

[1] W. Sparrow Simpson. *St. Augustine's Conversion*, p. 271.
[2] *De Lib. Arb.*, xi, 11.

faculties are distinct though inseparable "haec ergo tria
. . . animadverte separatim promuntiari, inseparabiliter
operari."[1]

Another psychological illustration of the Trinity is
given in *Conf.*, xiii, 11: "I wish that men would consider
the trinity they have within." Augustine refers here to
Being, Knowledge, and Will. Such analogies, he suggests, should be received with caution, for whether it is
the co-existence of these three that constitute a Trinity
in God or whether these three in Each Person, so that each
Person possesses all three, or whether both are true, it is
difficult to say, as it is beyond our understanding.

In connection with the teaching on the existence of
God, one fact, especially, must be emphasised, namely,
that all rational knowledge is ultimately knowledge of
God. Augustine is quite willing to admit that complete
knowledge of God is denied to human insight during
man's earthly life. The negative element in our idea of
Him is, doubtless, alone completely certain. It is logical
for us to believe that we have, and can have no adequate
idea of the way in which the different elements of divine
truth, which the reason beholds, are united to Him to
form the highest real unity. The thoughtful man, who
listens to the voice of reason, must believe that God's
incorporeal and changeless essence (essentia) far transcends all forms of relation and association that belong to
human thought. Consequently, the category of substance
applies to Him as little as do the rest.

[1] *Serm.* lii, 19, fin.

CHAPTER IX

REFLECTIONS ON THE TEACHING OF
ST. AUGUSTINE

PSYCHOLOGY, as a systematic inquiry into psychical processes and their conditions, may be said to owe its origin to Aristotle. His contribution to the subject is of real and continuing importance. In the first place, he is keenly conscious of the intimate interdependence of body and mind. We are indebted to him, also, for the systematic distinction of stages of mental processes, so arranged that each higher stage presupposes the existence of the lower. It is to Aristotle, also, that we are indebted for many important discourses on special psychological conditions, for his enumeration of the different principles of association and for his theory of dreams.

Aristotle, however, was unknown to the Christian Fathers. Their basis was Platonic, and this is specially true of Augustine although in practice there are to be found in his treatises, especially in the later dialogues, traces of Aristotelian influence. The working psychology of the Church, down to the rediscovery of Aristotle in the twelfth century, was Platonic.

Even in regions beyond the psychological, Augustine was the great teacher of the Middle Ages. The fundamentals of Christian and Neo-Platonic thought, as well as the ideas of Origen and Plotinus, unite in his philosophy. He also emphasises the thought of his time with creative energy on the need of salvation and the proclamation of this need by the Church. His doctrine becomes the philosophy of the Christian Church. Thus was formulated, in pregnant unity, the system which became the foundation of the scientific training of the European peoples, and in this way the Romanic and Germanic peoples entered upon the inheritance of the Greeks.

Augustine proves to be a forerunner in two diverse tendencies of medieval thought. In so far as he presents the doctrine of the Church as a scientific system he foreshadows the science of the Schools, that is Scholasticism; and in so far as he develops her Neo-Platonic tendencies, concentrating on the guidance of the individual, through knowledge, to blessed oneness of life with the deity, he points the way to medieval Mysticism.

The whole philosophical series of Augustine's writings is remarkable; he often conjoins, with much skill, the teaching of Plato and of St. Paul. His views on the relation between reason and faith are full of depth; he shows that faith is not only necessary in religion, but that it is the condition of man's understanding everything beautiful and great. Even friendship begins by an act of faith.[1]

Reason can arrive at truth only by being subordinate to faith. "It was necessary," he writes, "that God, through a kind of general clemency, should lower the authority of the divine intellect so as to make it the inmate of a human body."[2] Augustine asserts that faith strengthens reason and exults in rather than dethrones it.

Some of Augustine's apologetic writings, e.g. the *De Vera Religione, De Utilitate Credendi, Liber de fide rerum quae non videntur*, and the *Letter CXX to Consentius*, constitute him the great theorist of the Faith, and of its relation to reason. "He is the first of the Fathers," says Harnack, "who felt the need of forcing his faith to

---

[1] *De Util. Cred.*, 12, 13.
[2] *Cont. Acad.*, 19, 20.

reason."[1] He, who so often affirms that faith precedes the intelligent apprehension of the truths of revelation, explains, with greater clearness and definition and more precisely than anyone, the function of the reason in preceding and verifying the witness's claim to credence, and in accompanying the mind's act of apprehension.[2]

Although Augustine clearly recognised in the Will the inmost motive energy of human nature and regarded the striving after happiness as the impelling motive of all psychical functions, he remained, however, firmly convinced that the satisfaction of all this urge can be found only in "beholding divine truth." God is the highest good. Augustine emphasises the doctrine that God is the truth, and that a person enjoys truth by beholding it and resting in its contemplation. All incitement of the will is but the path to this peace, in which it rests. The final task of the will is to be silent at the gracious working of divine revelation. The will remains quiet when the vision of truth, produced from above, comes to it.

The teaching of Augustine, as the *Ethics* of Spinoza, includes ontology, psychology and deontology. In Augustine's writings we recognise that the Christian idea of the absolute causality of God, and the contemplative mysticism of the Neo-Platonists are united in common opposition to individualism of will. In the teaching of both, the same desire is in operation to develop the conception of man's sanctification as the working of God in him—as filled and illumined by the highest truth, as a contemplation of the One Infinite Being in which the will plays no part.

[1] *Hist. of Dogma* III, 97.
[2] *Letter to Consentius* IV, 3, 8, etc.

For temporal life, Augustine demands the full and continuous exertion of the struggling and active soul; with regard to eternity, he offers the prospect of the peace of becoming absorbed in divine truth. He, indeed, designates the state of the blessed as the highest of the virtues, as love (caritas). In his system we observe that the three Christian virtues, faith, hope, and love, are regarded as more important than the practical virtues of Greek ethics.

In the world of eternal blessedness, however, where the desires of the flesh and of this sinful will no longer need to be overcome, where love has no longer any want that craves satisfaction, there this love is nothing else than a God-intoxicated contemplation.

It is a remarkable fact, also that in this duality of the Augustinian ethics, old and new lie close together. The modern man appears endowed with great energy of will, which is necessary for the earthly life. The ethical judgment is transferred so as to make it apply to the inner disposition. In the conception of the highest goal of life, however, the ancient ideal of intellectual contemplation still prevails.

Thus we find in Augustine's doctrine itself an apparent contradiction of the individualism of the will. Accordingly, at a decisive stage an Aristotelian Neo-Platonic element maintains itself. This internal opposition unfolds itself in the development of the problems of the Middle Ages.

Augustine's profound knowledge of the operations of the will, and his perception of the extent to which this influenced even knowledge, led to the discovery of the principle that goodness and blessing, accordingly, final salvation also, coincided in the dependence of the will on

God. In this way he depressed intellectualism, and a wonderful blessing was shown to exist even in this world. "It is a good thing for me to cleave to God."

Of all the philosophers who preceded Descartes, Augustine is, perhaps, the man who had the clearest idea about the knowledge of the soul by means of the workings of the soul, and who had distinguished most clearly psychological phenomena from exterior phenomena. He has expressed himself upon the subject with the greatest earnestness and exactitude.

Augustine conceived, as Tertullian did, the human soul to be a substance, but the former regarded it at the same time as divisible and indivisible, present entirely in the whole body and also in every part of it. It was not a presence instead of another presence but a presence of action. He proved that it was distinct from human organism by showing the impossibility of making sensible ideas and also moral ideas to exist in a material object. The arguments he uses are precisely those which Plotinus has developed in his *Enneades*.

It was Plotinus, also, who furnished, to a considerable degree, to Augustine his principal arguments on the immortality of the soul, and in particular that which established the union of the soul with eternal truths, and that which bears upon the identity of the soul and life.

His views on the faculties of the soul are borrowed to a great extent from the Alexandrian philosopher. Before his time Plato had said that the soul is not passive, but active, in feeling; that the body alone suffers and that all the parts of the soul are taken up in perceiving it. Before his time he had, also, distinguished the spiritual memory from the sensible memory.

Augustine has spoken of the soul, as no other teacher.

If he explained transports of joy and admiration at the sight of the riches, order and beauty of the universe, he remained overpowered by feelings of awe when he contemplated the human soul, which contains all worlds within itself. He was fascinated and spell-bound by that unfathomable abyss wherein the Blessed Trinity is mirrored.

When he speaks of the depths of the soul, he has a definite intuition that God is to be found there and he has a desire to touch Him and to help us to touch Him also; hence his contempt for Epicurus. How could a man calling himself a philosopher so misunderstand the soul, its greatness and dominion over nature, as to make it the slave of the body?

It is only consistent with reason to believe that the body is not for the soul, but the soul for the body. All the noblest operations of the body, its activity and capacity for feeling, do not proceed from itself, but from life. And whence does life proceed but from the soul? The soul, then, is the higher and nobler part of man, the source of all his qualities and feelings, the centre of his well-being and happiness.

In connection with the science of man, Augustine's treatises are full of anecdotes which prove with what naïve curiosity he studied the things around him. He knew also how to ascertain the commonest facts of our nature.

Augustine's intellectual power is the result, in no small degree, of a ready memory. It proceeds also from a fruitful imagination. With Augustine, imagination always played an important part. Even in his later writings his comparisons, both amusing and solemn, but always natural and often very happy, abounded; these prepared the way for further thought and thus directed it in some mysterious way and enabled it to enter easily into his imagination. The same fact is even more conspicuous in the writings of his earlier years. The images he employs, at that time more freely and more graciously, give to his most abstract speculations a very special charm. These images are formed, unconsciously and almost in spite of himself, like those of a poet. It is greatly to his credit that he can be regarded as the first writer to describe operations of the imagination, and to develop a theory on the subject of dreams, hallucinations, ecstasy, and other abnormal phenomena. He displays remarkable originality in his analysis of the doctrine of the association of ideas and in his theory of the laws of memory.

Augustine mentions that no object can be beautiful and true unless there is in it absolute beauty and truth, and because in his own soul he finds only borrowed gleams of light on the subject, he urges that man must submit to the unchanging truth. But man's soul is active and intelligent as well as intelligible; it commands a view of nature and judges what is true. Now Divine Truth must be active, and God must be the Teacher, revealing His presence in those absolute standards, whereby the soul judges. We are reminded of the saying of Pascal: "Thou wouldst not be searching for Me, hadst thou not already found Me." We cannot desire what we do not already know: we judge of truth, because the Truth already abides in us: our love reveals the secret of His love, for "He is in our memory though we suspect it not." This aspect of psychology and metaphysics is the burden of Augustine's language about God as the Light and Truth within us. "Et ecce intus eras et ego foris et ibi Te quaerebam; mecum eras et tecum non eram."

One of the most remarkable features of Augustine's genius can be found in his certainty of instinct; remarkable in his almost supernatural judgment by which, whilst remaining a Platonist and in strict dependence on Plotinus in philosophy, he avoids the most dangerous pitfalls of Platonism; at one moment, he connects the teaching of his Greek masters, at another, he leaves unsolved those questions to which he realises that the Platonic method does not supply a key, as, for instance, many questions about the soul and its origin; at another time, he leaves some questions unsolved or in a state of uncertainty, such as certain great doctrines, for example his doctrine of illumination, which, by such a method, he could not bring to a more satisfactory degree of exactness without the risk of falling into grave error.

When Augustine asserts that our nature tends naturally to believe in God, he proceeds to explain that we are morally bound to love Him. We are free; we can see quite clearly where our happiness lies, and yet we voluntarily choose something else. All morality depends on liberty. In order to demonstrate this truth, Augustine wrote a treatise on free will. On the other hand, we do not think of a moral system without obligations and sanctions. May not the proposition therefore be transposed from "We tend naturally to God" to "We are bound to tend voluntarily to God"?[1]

It is at this stage that Augustine's superiority over the greatest Greek philosophers is most clearly seen. Plato and Plotinus, his former teachers, also say that the human soul desires God, that in Him alone does it find its truest equilibrium and perfect joy. God seems to them to be the supreme good and the man who would turn his back upon

[1] B. R. Gosselin in *A Monument to St. Augustine*, p. 233.

God and allow himself to be taken captive by the attractions of the sensible world is utterly foolish. We seek in vain, however, through the teaching of these philosophers, for a metaphysical notion of a real moral obligation. To them nature can only express a wish, an optative, it can never utter an imperative.

Maurice Blondel has written about the philosophy of Augustine:[1] "In the light of the problems discussed by contemporary psychologists, we can quickly realise what great advantage we can derive from the philosophy of Augustine in settling, in accordance with his spirit, the differences dividing the experimental school, the philosophy of intuition, and Idealist speculation, all equally extravagant, whereas in the philosophy of the saint we find a vital unity which allows each of these elements its legitimate share: hereditary fatalities, conscious experiences, rational elaboration, triumphs of the spiritual life, conflicts of the will, the influence of grace; all in admirable harmony in that stupendous tilting ground which is the soul, and in which all nature, the human will, and divine assistance compete together for the prize."

The debt of subsequent writers to St. Augustine
(a) Thomas Aquinas

The time which has elapsed between the teaching of a bishop of the fourth century and that of a schoolman of the thirteenth century renders the task of comparison very difficult. We cannot fail, however, to detect certain points of similarity in their writings. The remarkable doctrine on the subject of wisdom bequeathed to us by Augustine finds a place, with certain points of difference, in the system of Thomas Aquinas.

1 A Monument to St. Augustine, p. 333.

Every scholar recognises that the outstanding doctrine on which these two teachers are most agreed is that of grace. Jacques Maritain[1] says that Thomas Aquinas teaches the influence of free human will by grace and divine causality in such a way that even the free operation of our voluntary acts is caused by God as first cause and by ourselves as second; that we are a first (deficient) cause only for evil; that when he teaches how liberty (in the sense of autonomy) is the work of the grace of the Holy Ghost, it is the utterance of Augustine, and of St. Paul, to which we are listening.

The Augustinian proof of the existence of God, as previously stated, is found also in Thomas Aquinas's *Summa Theologica*.

With slight revision, the substance of Augustinian teaching on the subject of truth has passed into the teaching of Thomas Aquinas.[2]

Gardiel[3] writes: "The subjects on which they (Augustine and Thomas Aquinas) differ may be counted; it is impossible to number those on which they agree . . . the dumb ox . . . has devoured the whole spiritual substance of the eagle of Hippo . . . he has made it, as much as the teaching of Aristotle, the very substance of his own mind."

It must be mentioned, however, that when Thomas Aquinas adopts the teaching of Augustine, he by no means follows his leading slavishly. He has been influenced by his spirit and treats of some of the themes of the Latin Father from his own point of view, dealing with them frequently as a theological science.

[1] *A Monument to St. Augustine*, p. 215.
[2] See Boyer. *L'Idée de Vérité dans la philosophie de S. Augustin*, p. 108.
[3] *La Structure de l' Ame et l' Expérience Mystique*. Paris. 1927. p. 29–30.

(b) Descartes

A study of the writings of Descartes reveals the fact that a number of principles which are essential parts of his philosophy appear to be taken from St. Augustine.

Descartes evidently undermined the supremacy of Aristotle, but in so doing he restored the authority of Plato, and indirectly commended the teaching of Augustine. A number of writers go so far as to regard Augustine as the spiritual father of Descartes.

Comparing the teaching of Descartes on the subject of the soul with that of Augustine, it may be stated that to the former it is simply a substance, whereas for Augustine it is at the same time both a substance and a power. The teaching of Leibniz, who professed to have reformed the idea of the substance of the soul, is but a return to the idea of Augustine.

Directly or indirectly, Descartes certainly borrowed from him his method of internal observation and expressed this teaching in a remarkable manner.

A comparison of the early parts of the three principal works of Descartes: the *Discours de la Méthode*, the *Méditations*, and the *Principes de la Philosophie*, with the earlier writings of Augustine enable us to recognise in the theories of the "true originator of modern philosophy," as Descartes has been termed, a resurrection of the teaching of the father of all Christian philosophy.[1]

The *Recherche de la vérité*, written by Descartes in A.D. 1674, was the baptism of the Cartesian system into a theistic religion which borrowed its imagery from Augustine.

St. Augustine, when compared with Descartes, has been described as "Descartes minus the Method," for

[1] Erich Przywara in *A Monument to St. Augustine*, p. 252.

Descartes is, certainly, both methodical and clear. Descartes has combined psychology with physiology and thus brightened up his teaching on the human passions.

Some scholars hesitate to admit that Descartes came directly under the influence of St. Augustine; the fact remains, however, that his method condemned him to follow, in his treatment of metaphysics, the road prepared for him by Augustine.

Fénelon, comparing these two great writers, states:[1] "If an enlightened man collects in the books of St. Augustine all the sublime truths that this Father has there bestowed, as by chance, this extract made by selection would be very superior to the *Méditations* of Descartes, although these *Méditations* were the greatest effort of the spirit of the philosopher."

(c) Malebranche

Malebranche derived from St. Augustine, more than all other writers, that inspiration which pervades his brilliant discourses, which treat of God as the principal theme of all his researches.

From St. Augustine, indeed, Malebranche admits that he had borrowed his chief theory of the vision of God. For Malebranche, as for Augustine, truth is absolute; it is God Himself. Malebranche understands, in the same way as Augustine, that knowledge of God which men can enjoy.

He looks to Augustine to establish his distinction of the union of the soul with the body and of its union with God, and his teaching that the body cannot act upon the soul and that the soul is in direct communication with the Divine intelligence.

[1] Fénelon. *Lett. sur la Metaph.* Lett. 4.

Chiefly through the labours of Malebranche, the teaching of Augustine was diffused among all the religious orders of France, and was afterwards conveyed to England and to Italy.

(d) Other Writers

The best minds of every generation have admitted their debt to St. Augustine. Cassiodorus, in his enthusiasm for books and different kinds of learning, both sacred and secular, frequently turns to Augustine for support. Quotations from Augustine's writings and summaries of his teaching appear on every page of Isidore's *Etymologies.* The influence of Augustine's writings on Bossuet has been admirably described by M. Villemain.[1] To Augustine, Bossuet turns for a proof of the spirituality and immortality of the soul. Scotus Erigena learned to indulge in Speculation, as a second Plato, when there was none to inspire him save Augustine only. The humanism of the school of Chartres was Christian Platonism inspired directly by the teaching of Augustine. Hugh turned to his pages to enable him to formulate the distinction between faith and reason, between natural and supernatural; Richard studied his psychological system more closely than anyone before his day. Fénelon's remarkable statements about the marvels of memory find their genesis in Augustine's teaching on this subject.

The chapter of the history of Augustine's influence on the centuries is not yet closed. The greatest writers of past centuries alone have described this intellectual giant as the sovereign genius of his age and regard him with the love he deserved. It was not until after his death that this brilliant luminary of philosophy was appreciated. It was

---

[1] *Tabl. de l'éloq. crét. au quatrième siècle,* p. 504.

gradually realised more and more clearly that he was the pioneer who opened paths hitherto untrodden, and his reputation as a thinker has grown greater each passing century down to our own day. Evidence of his influence can be found in all directions. His teaching continues to inspire the souls of Christians and we believe will remain until the end of time.

CLOSING REMARKS

A GENERATION ago, when philosophical studies were coming into favour, it was thought that the thinker of this time had discovered new psychological truths and was leading the way to the investigation of new fields of research. It is evident, however, that it was St. Augustine, a theologian of the fourth century, who unfolded the principles of this science which has been regarded recently as comparatively new. With remarkable genius he has bequeathed to future generations a knowledge of these great principles which has served as a foundation, and on which subsequent psychologists have built.

It must be remembered, however, that St. Augustine was only a pioneer and, accordingly, has not bequeathed to posterity a complete system of philosophy. Neither he, nor the century in which he lived, experienced the need of it. His primary aim was to refute radical scepticism, to discover the spiritual in opposition to Manichaean Materialism, and to find a solution of the problem of the existence of evil. Augustine spent years in thinking out the possibility of a non-material reality and the compatibility of an imperfect universe with a perfect God. It occurred to him that if he could overcome these difficulties, his reasoning powers would work freely within the limits of the Christian faith; this realisation suggested that he has found the equivalent of a philosophy of life, and opened the way for reason to lead him to the true light.

Augustine developed certain truths, which served as a foundation for the progress of thought. After careful consideration of some of the essential elements of Platonism he placed them in a different setting. He bequeathed to posterity a philosophy, rich and full of possibilities; nevertheless, it must be confessed that it was incomplete.

It is not permissible, Harnack asserts, to compare St. Augustine with St. Athanasius: "Augustine was a loftier genius, a man of inexhaustible wealth of ideas and sentiment; Athanasius' greatness consisted in reduction. In the energy with which, from a multitude of divergent speculations claiming to rest on tradition, he gave exclusive validity to those in which the strength of religion lay, Augustine opened up a new view of the highest blessings and of human nature in the Church, and he scattered a thousand germs for the future."[1]

Augustine's psychology never completely neglects what is concrete; it is, perhaps, rather a moral service than a psychological; its teaching proceeds in a way quite different from that of the analytical psychology of Thomas Aquinas.

Augustine invented a new method of speculation, and this he expressed in the fascinating language of the deepest religious feeling, beyond which changed times and manners appear to be unable to go.

It is an amazing fact that St. Augustine has left scarcely a trace of his influence in the Eastern Church. That is its greatest calamity, says Harnack. Of course, the East, owing to its past, was less disposed to understand him than the Western Church, and it was at no time really inclined to accept instruction from its rival.[2]

Augustine has not composed a special treatise on psychology, at least we do not wish to give that description to his book on the Immortality of the Soul; but he

[1] *Hist. of Dogma*, III, p. 140.
[2] *Hist. of Dogma*, III, p. 150.

has, certainly, contributed a large number of beautiful and uplifting ideas on human nature. He felt the need of analysing these conceptions to ascertain the basis of some great moral or religious truth.

It is, in fact, one of the characteristics of his teaching that, when he is discussing some psychological question, he is often involved in some theological or moral problem. When he wishes to know whether his former passions still retain any control over his soul, with a view of getting rid of their influence, he analyses them most carefully and takes note, as a psychologist, of that weakness which he, as a moralist, tries to resist. It is often theological reasons rather than philosophical which lead him to his conclusions. If he treats of three species of concupiscence, viz., that of the flesh, that of the sight, and that of boasting, it is because he finds this division in the New Testament. After examination of the various solutions which he has learnt about the theory of the origin of the soul, if he is inclined to conclude that this is the result of the process of generation, it is because this interpretation appears to him easier to reconcile with the dogma of original sin.

Finally, rejecting pagan myths and distinguishing with a definite clearness God and His creatures, Augustine imparted to Greek philosophy, as represented by Plato, a new outlook. Although the doctrine on a single page of Augustine's writings may be Platonic in spirit yet the teaching appears in a new form, natural and modern, The connection between Christian theology and Greek philosophy is even clarified and humanised. At the same time it expands the scope of Greek thought.

Derived from the teaching of Aristotle and Plato, the doctrine of St. Augustine has become Christian philosophy and, as has been mentioned in the previous chapter, appears in certain important respects, in the treatises of Thomas Aquinas, Descartes, Bossuet, Fénelon and Malebranche.

Augustine did not believe that he was under any obligation to repudiate his philosophical culture because he had recovered his faith, nor was he afraid to acknowledge the part played by Plato and Cicero in his return to the Christian faith. Indeed, he was never ungrateful to his former instructors, but appropriated from them all knowledge which served to strengthen the foundations of his belief.

His merits soon exalted him to the highest rank amongst the Doctors of the Church. He was called upon to confront opponents, formidable by reason of their talents and influence, who tested his faith by their criticism; in order to oppose them effectively he never hesitated to meet them on their own ground, convinced that, as God is the author of reason as well as of faith, faith and reason can never contradict each other.[1]

What mostly impresses the reader in the study of his writings and influences him to indulge in growing admiration is that Augustine was, in his time, a great leader of education. It is a matter of thankfulness that his remarkable intellect did not stand in irreconcilable opposition to Christianity. On the other hand, he has bequeathed to mankind an ideal to realise and to excite a spirit of enthusiasm for inquiry and knowledge; he has awakened, in all religious people, an interest in those problems which appertain to the higher life of man. When he became a Christian, he brought all important questions under the clear light of that gospel, by which he had

[1] B. Roland-Gosselin in *A Monument to St. Augustine*, p. 228.

found peace for his soul. He united Christianity and culture in a way in accordance with his character, and exemplified in his own experience the truth of St. Paul's words, which, at a later time the members of the Church so often forgot—"All things are yours; and ye are Christ's; and Christ is God's."

Many of his statements and many figurative interpretations, if treated literally, are, no doubt, now out of date, and can be disproved; for the materials on which Augustine worked as exegete, historian, or psychologist afforded by no means a satisfactory foundation; the spirit which animated him, however, remains intact, because his work was neither that of a mere scholar, nor was it a mere system of ideas; it acquired a definite value because it transcends the occasion which has given birth to it. Other philosophers, no doubt, have constructed an apparently more technical and a more explicit metaphysic; others, again, have received wisdom no less supernatural; but none of them, doubtless, has been to the same extent such a philosophic critic of thought, and such an experienced analyst of the inner life. "Doctor of sin, conversion, grace, and justification, master of the mystic ways, philosopher of interior illumination, herald of charity, the Eucharist, Tradition, and the Catholic Church: so many aspects are united in him without confusion that he escapes all definition, all special classification."[1]

The spirit of Augustine continued to live and bear fruit long after Christian Africa had ceased to exist. It entered into the tradition of the Western Church and moulded the thought of Western Christendom so that even our civilisation bears the imprint of his genius.

[1] M. Blondel in *A Monument to St. Augustine*, p. 352.

However far we have travelled since the fifth century, and however much we have learnt from other teachers, the work of St. Augustine still remains an inalienable part of our spiritual heritage.

BIBLIOGRAPHY

P. Alfaric. *L'Evolution intellectuelle de Saint Augustin*. Paris	1918
Bardenhewer-Shahan. *Patrologie*. Freiburg	1908
I. de Beausobre. *Histoire critique de Manichée et du Manichaeisme*. Amsterdam	1734
H. Becker. *Augustin Studien zu seiner geistigen Entwicklung*. Leipzig	1908
E. Bersot. *Doctrine de S. Augustin sur la liberté et la providence*. Paris	1843
C. Bigg. *The Christian Platonists of Alexandria*. Oxford	1913
C. Bindemann. *Der heilige Augustinus*. Berlin	1844
M. Blondel. Art. "The Latent Resources in St. Augustine's Thought" in *A Monument to St. Augustine*. London	1930
G. Boissier. Essay in the *Rev. des deux mondes*. Paris	1888
C. Boyer. *L'idée de Vérité dans la philosophie de Saint Augustin*. Paris	1920
C. Boyer. *La Formation de Saint Augustin*. Paris	1920
W. Bright. *Anti-Pelagian Treatises of St. Augustine*. Oxford	1880
F. C. Burkitt. *The Religion of the Manichees*. Cambridge	1925
M. Le R. Burton. *The Problem of Evil*. Chicago	1909
E. Cuthbert Butler. *Western Mysticism*. London	1922
Catholic Encyclopaedia. London	1907
Combés. *S. Augustin et la culture classique*	1927
W. Cunningham. *S. Austin and his place in the history of Christian thought*. London	1886
C. Dawson. "The City of God" in *A Monument to St. Augustine*. (London.) Sheed & Ward	1930
E. de Pressensé. Art. "Augustine" in *Dictionary of Christian Biography*. (London) Murray	1877
C. A. Dubray. *Introductory Philosophy*. New York	1913
J. E. Erdmann. *History of Philosophy*. (English translation.) London	1893
R. Eucken. *The Problem of Human Life*. London	1909
A. M. Fairbairn. *The place of Christ in modern theology*. London	1893
F. de S. Fénelon. *Lettres sur la métaphysique*. Paris	1830
M. Ferraz. *La Psychologie de Saint Augustin*. Paris	1862
Gardiel. *La Structure de l'Ame et l'Expérience Mystique*. Paris	1927
J. Gibb and W. Montgomery. *The Confessions of Augustine*. Cambridge	1908
E. Gilson. *Introduction à l'étude de Saint Augustin*. Paris	1929
E. Gilson. "The future of Augustinian metaphysics" in *A Monument to St. Augustine*. London.	1930
T. R. Glover. *Life and Letters in the Fourth Century*. Cambridge.	1901

B. R. Gosselin. "St. Augustine's System of Morals" in *A Monument to St. Augustine*. London   1930

C. Gore. Art. "Victorinus" in *Dictionary of Christian Biography*. (London.) Murray   1911

L. Grandgeorge. *St. Augustin et Le Néo-Platonisme*. Paris   1896

Sir. W. Hamilton. *Lectures on Metaphysics and Logic*. Edinburgh   1860

A. Harnack. *History of Dogma*. (English translation.) London   1896

A. Harnack. *Dogmengeschichte*. Tübingen   1922

H. Hoffding. *History of Philosophy*. (English translation.) London   1895

W. R. Inge. *The Philosophy of Plotinus*. London.   1918

W. James. *The Varieties of Religious Experience*. London   1902

Otto Klemm. *Geschichte der Psychologie*. Leipzig.   1906

G. Kruger. Art. "Augustine" in *Encyclopædia Britannica*   1929

T. A. Lacey. Art. "Augustine" in *Encyclopædia Britannica*   1929

J. Laidlaw. *The Bible Doctrine of Man*. (Revised edit.) Edinburgh   1895

M. B. Legervie. *Augustinus eine Psychographie*. Bonn   1925

J. B. Lightfoot. *Notes on the Epistles of St. Paul*. London   1895

J. Locke. *An Essay concerning Human Understanding*. London   1812

Jules Martin. *Saint Augustin*. Paris   1901

W. Montgomery. *St. Augustine: Aspects of his life and thought*. London   1914

W. Montgomery. "St. Augustine's attitude to psychic phenomena" Art. in *Hibbert Journal*. p. 92. London   1926

F. W. H. Myers. *Human Personality*. London   1903

J. F. Nourrisson. *La Philosophie de Saint Augustin*. Paris   1865

W. O'Connor. *The concept of the human soul*. Milwaukee   1921

R. L. Ottley. *Studies in the Confessions of Augustine*. London   1919

G. Papini. *Saint Augustine*. London   1930

T. J. Parry. *Augustine and Platonism*. Leipzig   1913

G. Philips. *La raison d'être du mal d'après saint Augustin*. Louvain   1927

E. Portalié. Art. "S. Augustin" in *Dictionnaire de Théologie Catholique*   1902

J. B. Pratt. *The Religious Consciousness*. (New York.) Macmillan   1921

E. Przywara. "St. Augustine and the Modern World" in *A Monument to St. Augustine*. London   1930

H. Rashdall. *Ideas and Ideals*. Oxford   1928

J. B. Reeves. "St. Augustine and Humanism" in *A Monument to St. Augustine*. London   1930

J. Rickaby. "The Manichees as Saint Augustine saw them." London   1925

A. Robertson. Art. "Aurelius Augustinus" in *Dictionary of Christian Biography*. (London.) Murray   1911

P. Schaff. *The Life and Labours of St. Augustine.* (London.) Bagster 1854

P. Schaff. *St. Augustine, Melancthon, Neander.* London 1886

P. Schaff. *History of the Christian Church.* Edinburgh 1884

W. S. Simpson. *St. Augustine's Conversion.* London 1930

W. S. Simpson. *The Letters of St. Augustine.* London 1919

W. S. Simpson. *St. Augustine on the Spirit and the Letter.* London 1925

J. Stortz. *Die Philosophie des Augustinus.* Freiburgh 1882

A. G. Tansley. *The new Psychology.* London 1922

F. R. Tennant. *Philosophical Theology,* Vol. I. Cambridge 1928

W. Thimme. *Augustins geistige Entwickelung in den ersten Jahren nach seiner Bekehrung.* Berlin 1908

R. H. Thouless. *An Introduction to the Psychology of Religion.* Cambridge 1923

W. P. Tolley. *The Idea of God in the Philosophy of St. Augustine.* New York 1930

F. Ueberweg. *History of Philosophy.* London 1872

E. Wallace. *Aristotle's Psychology.* Cambridge 1882

B. B. Warfield. Art. "Augustine" in *Dictionary of Religion and Ethics.* Edinburgh 1919

R. M. Wenley. Art. "Augustianism" in *Dictionary of Philosophy and Psychology.* London 1902

F. Woerter. *Die Unsterblichkeitslehre in den philosophischen Schriften Augustins.* Freiburg 1880

T. V. Zahn. *Bible, Science and Faith.* (French Translation.)

INDEX

Printed in Great Britain for ELLIOT STOCK, *Publisher*, 2 PATERNOSTER BUILDINGS, LONDON, E.C., *by* SIMSON & CO., LTD., HERTFORD.